EVERYTHING WILL BE OKAY

Your support means the world

DANA BUCKMIR

Disclaimer
This is a work of creative nonfiction. The events are portrayed to the best of my memory. While all the stories in this book are true, some names and identifying details have been changed to protect the privacy of the people involved.

DEDICATION

For Peter, who taught me that when life gets you down, bike to the beach. If that doesn't work, drink a beer. I hope Heaven has an unlimited supply of sunshine and PBRs.

ACKNOWLEDGMENTS

To Louise and all the members of the memoir writing group, thank you. Your feedback, encouragement and guidance have helped strengthen my confidence and craft.

To Katy, for always being there for me day and night to make sense of the mess that is life. I'm not sure I would have made it through this year without you.

To my mother, for supporting my writing dreams and taking the time to objectively critique the difficult content presented in this book. I love you.

To Amanda, the grammar queen, for your critical eye and attention to detail.

To Lucky, my faithful companion, who has been with me through every stage of the writing process. I'm truly lucky to have you by my side.

To all the women who have experienced domestic violence and narcissist abuse: I see you, I hear you, I am you. You're not alone.

"And in the end, we were all just humans…
drunk on the idea that love,
only love, could heal our brokenness."

-F. Scott Fitzgerald

CHAPTER 1

I met a medium in a Starbucks expecting a crystal ball and perhaps a package of tarot cards. Choosing a table in the corner for privacy, I took off my jacket and hung it on the back of the chair. I reached into my bag and took out a notebook, some pens, and placed them on the table alongside my phone. The time displayed on the screen signaled that I had ten minutes until she arrived. Waiting in anticipation for my guest, I opened the notebook and began to prepare for the meeting, recording the date at the top of a page. The writer in me appreciated a new notebook. I imagined that the way I viewed the crisp, blank pages waiting to be filled with words was similar to how an artist looked at a blank canvas before wrapping it in color.

I took in my surroundings, paying attention to the music coming from the speakers in an attempt to deafen my racing thoughts. It was an acoustic medley that seemed louder than it should be, forcing the people around me to yell to hear each other over the cacophony of sound. I removed a lavender essential oil from my bag and rubbed a few drops on my wrist clockwise in a circular motion breathing in the sweet, floral aroma. These were grounding strategies that my therapist, Aimee, had recommended as part of a toolkit for when I get anxious. I could hear her voice instructing me: *Take an overall body assessment. Start in the lower half of your body and clench your toes. Tighten all the muscles moving up your body to your head. Then release the tension and relax.* Sometimes her suggestions worked and sometimes they didn't. Focusing on something other than myself was almost always effective.

The crowded atmosphere of the bustling coffee shop was the perfect place to people-watch. A line formed comprised of several people impatiently awaiting their morning caffeine fix. Others settled into work with their laptops open, donning focused expressions on their faces that meant business. I imagined their names, their lives and their secrets. Did the woman in the smart pants suit tell her husband that she was going to the office, but was really meeting her lover? Did the young girl with the tight jeans and the crop top find the courage to tell her boyfriend that she missed her period and might be pregnant? Creating scenarios for strangers placed the focus on external elements rather than my inner monolog.

I didn't give her any information about me or even a physical description. All I had was her first name, Lauren, followed by 'medium' listed in my phone contacts. We communicated via text message the week before to set up a time and location. When she entered knowing exactly what table to approach, I thought *this woman might just be the real deal.* Of course, she knew who she was meeting. She was a medium after all. The eyeshadow brushed above her eyelids matched her light blue nursing scrubs. She had a softness in her eyes that comes from a career built on a life dedicated to helping others. The red, curly hair cascading down her back gave her an effervescent look. She extended her hand to reach mine, exposing a multitude of colorful patterns on her long acrylic nails. There was a familiarity in her smile and a warmth in the way she held my hand gently while we shook.

Lauren explained how our session would transpire.

"There is a realm between the living and the spirit world," she began. It's kind of like if you picture a big arena. There are people waiting along the fence to get in. We're sitting on the bleachers. The people waiting are close enough to see, but far enough that we can't make them out. We can hear them faintly, but not enough to understand what they're saying. They approach the gate to enter the stadium but can only enter if we invite them."

I nodded, furiously scribbling notes about an arena and bleachers with spirits waiting at the gate. Then, I put my pen down, deciding it was better to just listen.

She continued. "We have to be careful who we let in. The afterlife isn't much different than the world that we exist in. Everything isn't always what it seems. Some spirits are demons with bad intentions. They may try to impersonate your loved one to get access. Evil only wants to harm you. It's my job as a gatekeeper to assess them and decide if they're really who they say they are. I do this by asking questions to check their identity and getting feedback from you for validation. As far as protection…" She placed a cross on the left side of the table and crystals on the right. "These medallions will keep us safe."

"What happens if someone gets through who isn't supposed to? What then?" Memories of my very Catholic mother finding a Ouija Board under my bed and subsequently subjecting my eleven-year-old self to a lecture on religion had warned me of the consequences that could result from playing with anything that wasn't Godly.

"I'll make sure that doesn't happen. Don't worry. You're in a safe space," she said with a comforting smile, clasping my hand firmly as a sign of reassurance.

And although I had only met Lauren a few minutes before, I trusted her. Something about her being a nurse, her kind demeanor and the instant comfort level between us made me believe that she knew what she was doing. So I eased into the moment, putting my faith in the universe and the medium I met that morning in Starbucks to evaluate my past and determine my future.

"Do you have any more questions?"

A few questions came to mind like: *Who was this crazy woman who claimed she could communicate with the dead? When did my life become so messed up that I was seeking guidance from the spirit world?* And more importantly: *Should I ask her for the Powerball numbers?*

I decided that none of those questions were appropriate to ask, and so I responded, "No questions." As soon as the two words escaped my mouth I wondered if Lauren could tell I was lying.

"Are you ready to proceed?"

"Yes," I said, buckling up my invisible seatbelt in preparation for our journey into the unknown realm of the beyond.

Closing her eyes and reopening them seconds later, Lauren asked, "Who is the man with pain in his bones?"

Pain in his bones? I had no idea who she was referring to.

"You just saw him."

I wrinkled my brow. My eyes searched left and right.

"He's an older man."

She's talking about Peter. How did she know that? Jesus H. Christ, why did she bring him up? Peter was my best friend who lived in Fort Lauderdale. There was an age gap of over twenty-years between us, so he was more like a father than a friend, if you had the type of father who drank Pabst Blue Ribbons, rode his bike to the beach, and told wild stories about life tending bar at the Elbo Room. We looked out for each other. I had just gotten back from a monthly visit to see Peter. The trip ended with the knowledge that his stage 4 cancer diagnosis had spread throughout his body to his bones. The initial diagnosis that began in Stage 1 had loomed over our heads like a dark cloud for months, neither he nor I had wanted to address it because then it would become real, and that pain was something that we couldn't bear. So we did what any person would do when they didn't want to deal with something; we practiced avoidance. We resolved not to talk about it, silently wishing it away and ignorantly believing that if we didn't utter the dreaded C-word, it didn't exist.

The last time I saw Peter was just a few weeks ago on my most recent trip to South Florida. He was admitted to the hospital on the final day of the visit. There was nothing the doctors could do. So I sat by his bedside and held his hand, tears streaming down my face, thinking how cruel death was to rob the world of this remarkable person. My person. My friend. I looked at the frail man that he now was, remembering the vibrant life he once had. Tubes were hooked up to him, and I could see his breathing was labored. The monitor beeped periodically. It was time to say goodbye, and he didn't have much of it. He opened his eyes and called my name. I leaned over him, smiling. He said, "why don't you go to the beach?" I nodded, unable to hold back sobs. I pressed my lips to his forehead and kissed him. "Bye, Babe," he said, the last words I would ever hear him utter. That afternoon, I left on a plane to go back to Connecticut. While I was leaving South Florida, Peter was leaving this earth.

Coming to terms with Peter's death was too much for me to register, so I responded how I usually did when something was uncomfortable and difficult to process. "I don't want to talk about that."

"Of course," she said, respecting my decision. "I'll push the image away. Let's move on."

Lauren's mention of Peter surprised me, but I was still skeptical of her abilities. I really wanted to speak with her about my father, who had passed away the previous Christmas. "Can you communicate with my dad?"

"I'll try. What's his name?"

Shouldn't she know that already?

She said my father's name aloud. "If you are here, please reveal yourself. Come forward and give us a sign."

She looked away in a far-off gaze and grew silent, as if she went somewhere outside of the noise and the chatter. I sat patiently waiting. Seconds felt like minutes and then she spoke, "I'll shoot him. Don't think I won't. I have the right to protect the ones I love, especially if he comes in my house."

I jumped, startled by the aggressive tone and overall mannerism coming from Lauren.

"That fucking son of a bitch. If he thinks he's going to get away with it, he has another thing coming."

I looked around to see if anyone noticed the change in Lauren's behavior, in addition to the expletives firing from her mouth like one of the guns my father had owned. But the people around us continued drinking their caffeinated beverages, undisturbed by the outburst. The way that everyone carried on unbothered made me question if I had imagined what I had just witnessed. *You're losing it, Dana. Maybe the anxiety had gotten the best of you.*

But Lauren's next words made me realize that this was indeed happening. "I'll kill him. I'll kill the bastard for doing what he did to you. If that guy thinks he'll get away with it, he has another thing coming." *Okay, I definitely didn't imagine this.* I looked around to a room full of people unphased by any of her antics, while a scream began to build up and rise inside me. I had to say something.

"Excuse me," I interrupted her rant. The redness that had taken residence in her face began to fade back to her normal complexion, and her features that were just seconds ago so tense began to relax. "Why are you talking to me like that? I really don't think it's professional for you to speak like that. This isn't what I signed up for." I stood from my chair, started to collect my notebook, pens and phone, and quickly threw them in my bag. *I knew this was a bad idea. I can't believe I just spent one hundred dollars to sit here and have this woman, not only swear like a sailor, but threaten me. What kind of scam is she running?*

"Please, Dana." Lauren motioned for me to sit down. Her voice was calm and soothing. Her face was concerned. "I'll explain."

I had already come this far; it didn't make sense to leave without at least getting some sort of explanation for this madness, so I sat back down and opted to hear her out.

"I'm sorry," she said sweetly. "That wasn't me talking."

"It wasn't you? I don't understand. It looked like you. Your mouth was moving and words were coming out."

"Well, it was me, but it wasn't me." She smiled like she had had this conversation before.

"I'm confused," I said, thinking this might be too much for me to handle and maybe that is why it took me so long to consider going to a medium in the first place.

"It was your father."

"My father?" I said in disbelief.

"The dead speak. I convey their messages exactly as they relay them to me."

Piecing together what she said, it made perfect sense: the hostility, the reference to guns, defending the house, the intimidating tone. Come to think of it, it sounded exactly like my father. How could I not have known that? More importantly, how could she have known that's how he used to talk? He had been gone for over a year now, but Lauren managed to bring him back into the room.

It was a Saturday morning when I got the call from my grandfather. I had been living in Florida for six years. My plan was to go to the dog park as I typically did every weekend. I had the Christmas packages for my father in the car ready to be dropped off at the post office. Seeing my grandfather's number appear on the screen, I thought it was unusual for him to call so early. Generally, we spoke in the afternoon and it was only 8am. I knew it must be important.

"Good morning."

"Dane, your dad died last night."

Who knew that only six words strung together could make such an impact and change the course of my life? Four months later, I was back in Connecticut moving into the house where my father had died. The grief of losing a parent is always devastating, but mine was maximized by living with his ghost. All of his belongings filled the house. Everything was left untouched. The little red light blinked on the answering machine, indicating a message. I pushed the button to listen. The voice was mine giving my father a hard time for not calling me back.

"Hellooooo. I've tried you a few times, but you must be out on a yacht in Ibiza if you can't call me back."

Our nightly ritual was to talk on the phone, and it was something sacred that should only be broken if an elaborate excursion took precedence over the one receiving the phone call. The yacht was a new one I just introduced. Other excuses we had previously used included a safari adventure in Africa and a ski trip in the Alps. Anything that was over the top would suffice. We were both a bit dramatic, and sarcasm had been passed down in my DNA. I wish he had been on a yacht or some type of adventure, but the truth is that that night he was busy dying on a lethal cocktail of pills and booze, which rendered him unavailable to come to the phone. I was left in this space with all of his memories and life possessions to do with as I wished. But what do you do with them?

Every time I tried to get rid of something, my grandfather would intervene.

The urine-soaked couch from the dog that my father couldn't take out. "You should keep that. It's a good couch," my grandfather said. "Where will you sit?"

A basket of dad's socks, worn and caked with cigarette smoke. "I wouldn't get rid of those. Connecticut winters are cold. You never know when you might need some socks."

I learned to throw things out little by little without announcing them to my grandfather. I knew he felt like every item that was discarded represented an artifact from a life that we couldn't get back.

I had moved into a life that wasn't my own. A mausoleum that I was expected to exist in. A freeze frame that was stuck on pause. One that I never imagined would be mine or would have chosen for myself. To say that this was challenging was an understatement. I was uprooted. I was isolated. I had no idea what I was going to do in this new stage of my life. I had the pressure of being there for my grandfather. I was the closest thing to my father that he had left. My grandfather needed me to call him every day and go visit him as my father did. He needed me to do the things that he did with my father, like plant tomatoes, cook and make trips to the store. I don't think he ever recovered from my father's death. Do we ever get over a loss? The pain didn't get easier. He just learned to live with it.

"A father should never have to bury his child," he said, looking down at the ground and shaking his head in disbelief. "It's not supposed to happen this way. He should be planning my funeral. Not me planning his."

I put my hand on his shoulder to console him. There were no words to alleviate his suffering. In that moment I realized that life strips away our expectations, robbing us from the false illusion that we actually control our destiny.

———⟨∞⟩———

"Oh, I didn't realize," I said to Lauren apologetically.

"No need to apologize. I know this is new to you."

"This is surreal. It's a lot to take in." I exhaled deeply, sighing out the nervous energy and resolving to proceed. "Well, I guess we have enough information to invite him in." I laughed, using humor to counteract the awkwardness of the situation.

"Yes, I think so," she said smiling.

As is human nature, I wanted more. "Can you ask him to tell you something that no one would know?" Clearly, I was grappling with some major trust issues if at this point I still needed confirmation of my father's presence, but Lauren understood and gingerly complied.

"Of course." She went to that distant place again with the far-off look and silence ensued, listening intently to someone that wasn't physically there.

"What is he saying?"

She raised her finger indicating that I should hold on for a minute and continued to take everything in before speaking. Then, she said, "Your father asked me to tell you that he sees you in the bathroom smelling his cologne."

I could feel the color drain from my face. My chest tightened. My pulse raced. It was hard to breathe. I felt winded, like someone had just punched me in the gut. How could she know that?

My father's colognes stayed in the center section of the medicine cabinet. I used the space around them, respecting that their residence had seniority over my toiletries. The cabinet was just one example of how I built my new life around his old one. For the most part, the colognes sat untouched on the three tiers of shelving, but from time to time, when I would miss him and wanted to feel like a part of him was with me. I'd open up the cabinet, choose one out of the dozen in the collection, take the top off and breathe deeply from the bottle. With each long inhale, the grief subsided and the memories of him returned with the scent of his musk. Each of the bottles represented a piece of my father that I could visit, preserved in protective glass. I never told a soul that I huffed my father's cologne. It was too embarrassing to admit out loud. In a way, the ritual was something sacred that I shared with my father. No one else had to know, and no one should have, but this woman – she knew. There was no logical or worldly explanation for her knowledge, other than my father was communicating to me, through her. After that, I was a believer.

"Is there anything he wants to say?"

"He says he's proud of you and loves you." A wave of emotion rushed over me. The tears flowed uncontrollably, and I wept like a child who had lost her father, because I was. I sobbed in my hands in the middle of a Starbucks and didn't care who saw.

"He wants you to know that he's always with you," she continued. "Even when you don't feel his presence. He's there."

Sniffling and wiping away my tear-soaked face, I said, "Hopefully, he's not always here," using humor to diffuse the intensity of the moment. "There are some things I don't need him to see."

Lauren smiled and waited patiently for me to compose myself. "It looks like you have something on your mind," she said.

"It's just...I don't understand. Why did he leave me?" The birthday card I received from him only a month before he ended his life read *Happy Birthday Dane. I'll always be here for you.* But he was wrong. He wasn't here for me. I was here alone, expected to take ownership of a life that he couldn't live anymore and a house that wasn't supposed to be mine in a state I swore I'd never come back to. Connecticut. Once again, I felt abandoned.

"He says he's sorry. If he could do it again, he'd do it differently. He just didn't want to be in pain anymore, sweetie."

"What am I supposed to do now?"

"He knows that life hasn't been easy for you. Always remember that you're strong and resilient. You can meet any challenges you face in life. You're a survivor."

"Who was he talking about shooting before, and why did he mention protecting the house?"

"You know, sometimes we can't take things said too literally. Words can represent feelings of unresolved emotions, but don't necessarily correspond to actions." Lauren said.

I nodded, still wondering what his initial message could mean, but figured I'd leave it for another time. This had been an oversaturation of emotions and information for one morning.

"One more thing," she said. "He wants you to be happy."

I smiled at the simplicity of the comment that every parent wants for their child. The idea of happiness, although one of the most significant emotions, was one that I longed for. I didn't know what happiness looked like, but it was the one thing in my life that I was lacking. A void that made me feel incomplete and empty, one I needed so desperately to fill.

"Do you have any questions for me, sweetie?"

My head was spinning. I had so many questions, but one burned in my heart begging to be released. I took a deep breath and with a shaking voice asked, "will I ever find love?" I felt vulnerable as soon as I said it and wished I could take it back.

Lauren didn't hesitate. "You will," she blurted out joyously.

I couldn't believe my ears. I had given up on ever finding love. To hear these words renewed my hope.

"Really?" I said tearing up again and wondering when I became such an emotional wreck. "How will I know when I do?"

"You'll get a message. There will be an undeniable chemistry that you'll feel compelled to explore. You'll share the same insights, same dreams, same interests as if you're looking in a mirror and seeing the image of yourself reflected back from your kindred spirit."

Our time was up. Lauren stood, gave me a big hug and told me I could call her anytime. "Take care of yourself, sweetie,"

I watched her walk away, dumbfounded from what I just experienced. I wanted to share it with someone. Anyone. So I turned to the table next to me and said in a giddy tone, "I'm going to fall in love."

The two old women looked at me cautiously, smiled and nodded. One said, "that's nice dear" and then quickly returned to sipping her mochaccino and conversation so as not to engage with the random stranger who had been hysterically crying for the past forty-five minutes and now was oversharing about her love life. I grabbed my coat and the rest of my things and exited the coffee shop, feeling lighter. My heart was full with the promise of what the future would bring.

CHAPTER 2

Demons come in many forms. Mine appeared in the shape of a 6-foot man. Athletic build with green eyes, brown hair and a devilish smile. Erik Becker came into my life when I had almost given up on online dating. I say almost, because thinking back now, our connection was ironic for a couple of reasons. The first was that I was promoting *Plenty of Laughs* based on my online dating experience, but had vowed to never meet anyone online again. My time navigating the online dating waters had taught me that connecting with someone organically was the best route. The second being that technically I met Erik online, although not on a dating app. We met on Facebook. The social network seemed safer since on that platform you're linked to actual people you know in your friends list, as opposed to some random connection in cyberspace. Facebook profiles give you a panoramic picture of who the person is from their posts and history, rather than just a snapshot of what they put in a dating profile.

Erik's friend request was one of the many that I accepted in the hopes of trying to build a brand. As a first-time author, I figured that each connection I made was one more person that saw my name and associated it with my book. My philosophy:

More contacts equal more exposure. I blindly accepted every-one without vetting them.

Our first exchanges weren't anything memorable. In fact, I wasn't initially impressed by him, which explains why it took me over a month to respond to his unabating attempts to make contact through Facebook chats with messages like, "Hi," "Hey beautiful," "Hello." But eventually his message got my attention.

How are you? When are we cuddling together?

Who was this guy that I'd never spoken to, let alone met, asking me to cuddle? I tapped on the small circle with his pic-ture and selected "View profile." His Facebook page showed that he lived a few towns away from me. It looked like he was a bartender. He liked to bake. Lots of food posts, a few out-door pics, and some funny memes on his feed. Nothing overtly incriminating. Maybe it was out of boredom or curiosity or the genuine belief to see the good in everyone, but I replied.

Do I know you?

Not yet

Really? He was a confident one. I took the bait, deciding to play along.

Cuddling huh?
Is that a service you provide?

The three dots at the bottom of the page indicated he was typing a response.

Absolutely free of charge.
It comes with a complimentary back
massage and foot rub.

He set himself up with that one. I had no choice but to let him have it.

> *It sounds like you're pulling a*
> *Weinstein.*

Um no.
Nothing Harvey Weinstein about me. Lol

Did I detect a slight irritation? Or was he just asserting himself? It was so hard to determine through text. Messages got lost in translation when unaccompanied by gestures, facial expressions or tone. You never knew with the "lols" that were liberally sprinkled to give the appearance of a light-hearted statement.

His proposition sounded exactly like something Harvey Weinstein would do.

> *He offered massages as a way*
> *to lure women.*

Well I can't offer you a movie deal

> *That's too bad.*
> *I might have considered it for*
> *a movie deal.*

What was wrong with me? I was flirting shamelessly with the guy I just compared to a sexual predator.

We can definitely make a movie.
You can be my co-star.

Here we go. This is where he incorporates sexual inuendo.

> *What kind of movie are we*
> *going to make?*

I asked, waiting to hear what I already expected.

An action film with a lot of sexual tension.

Well, that was disappointing. I thought maybe he wouldn't go there, but of course, he did.

> *You're a weird dude.*

The inappropriateness of his replies pervaded through the text, prompting me to call him out. It was odd that he felt so comfortable introducing sexual overtones so early in our conversation.

Okay. Sorry you assumed that.
Have a good night.

I had had many conversations via messenger and learned too often that men got nasty when they felt rejected. Erik didn't show any signs of aggression. He bowed out in a somewhat graceful manner.

Erik was the poster child for "sliding into DMs." He disappeared for a few weeks and then reappeared in my direct messages with a "Hey there, gorgeous" as if we talked every day. This went on for a while, and then one day he commented on my video about coffee dates with a long, thoughtful response:

Asking someone to a coffee date is the equivalent of typing 'hey' as your opening line. Where's the effort? Let's meet at this coffee shop at this time takes zero effort, thought, or planning. This doesn't mean to go and reserve a table for two at the most exclusive restaurant in town for someone you just matched with either. The effort should start before the first date is even discussed. Ask questions, answer questions, crack jokes, get to know that person and see if there is chemistry. You might have learned through conversation that she loves seafood, book a table for two by the water. To me this is all common sense, interact online as you would in real life. Put the effort in. It's usually worth it.

Reading this comment on my Facebook post made me reconsider my previous judgment of Erik. Maybe I had given him a hard time for no reason. He had only asked me to cuddle, afterall. It's not like he asked me to have sex with him. I couldn't help but notice that he was trying. He was taking an interest in my work. Unlike a lot of the guys I had spoken to, he was capable of making intelligent points that contributed to the conversation. I should give him a chance.

My phone vibrated and the chat icon indicated that I had a message from Erik.

Humor is my number one turn on. You take the cake.
I really enjoy your videos. Very entertaining.

Erik had not only done his research, but he appreciated the qualities that he learned about me. He had captivated my interest. I was willing to learn more about him. I made a bet with Mia, or you might call it a social media experiment, that if I commented on his post about lobster rolls he'd ask me out on a date.

Mia and I had met while teaching in South Florida. She had become one of my best friends, and although there was a physical distance between us since I moved back to Connecticut, we talked daily. She was the one that knew everything about my dating history, just as I knew hers. Every dating decision I made was run by Mia. Erik was no different.

I typed in his name in the search bar, which directed me to his page. Scrolling down to the picture of a hot lobster roll with butter and a cold draft beer, I typed two words in the comment box, "I want," followed by a drooling emoji, and pressed the blue send arrow. I didn't have to wait long. He answered with multiple lobster GIFs and a message. "Now that you have an insatiable craving for lobster. Let's do dinner tomorrow. I know a place that makes the best lobster rolls."

And just like that, I agreed to a date, believing that if I embraced it with an open heart, the universe would give me exactly what I needed.

CHAPTER 3

He was late. I waited in the parking lot sitting on the dock, my legs extended over the water. The boats swayed subtly, rocking from side to side as a wave rolled under them. Honking swans circled anxiously. I leaned over to get a better view of them, reflecting on the irony of how something that appeared innocuous could be menacing. Children ordered ice cream cones in the shack next to the restaurant. The humidity had died down and a subtle breeze from the harbor cooled the air. It was a picturesque New England summer night. The restaurant was an impressive selection for a first date. Romantic water views. White table cloths. But his tardiness was frustrating.

"Ma'am, you can't sit there," a worker said. I got up from the dock, obeying his request. I pulled out my phone and looked at the time displayed on the home screen. He was now fifteen minutes late. I opened up my messages, looked for Mia's name and started typing.

If this guy stands me up, I'll swear off dating forever.

Mia's text came in immediately.

He won't.

I responded with a picture of a nun.

I can always join a convent.

Mia laughed with an emoji.

Do you want to call me?

A ding indicated I had another message. This time from Erik.

I'll be there in 5 minutes

Phew, I wasn't being ghosted.

He's on his way. Talk to you later.

Have a great time, soul sister. Love you.

A jeep blasting *Foo Fighters* pulled into the parking lot. *That had to be him.* I put my phone in my bag and walked toward the beat-up Wrangler, noticing the rust. The top was down. The doors were off. Erik was fixing his hair in the rear-view mirror, pushing the strands that had been windblown to the side.

Approaching the passenger side, I yelled into the vehicle. "Who are you trying to look good for?"

He turned to me and smiled. "You of course, daaaling," he said, drawing out the "a" and dropping the "r," adding to the theatrics.

At well over 6 feet, he was taller than I envisioned. He wore a long-sleeved white linen dress shirt, unbuttoned at the top. The sleeves were rolled up and folded. His shorts were a salmon khaki and he sported boat shoes. He looked like he was ready for a trip to the Vineyard.

"Nice to meet you," I said, giving him a hug.

"Thank you for waiting. I'm sorry I was late. I lost track of time."

Looking at the similarity between his pastel shorts and mine, I said, "It looks like we had the same idea."

"Matchy-matchy," he said. "You look absolutely gorgeous, by the way." He grabbed my hand and twirled me around, turning me to face him. "I like to get the goodnight kiss out of the way in the beginning of the date to avoid an awkward anticipation that might take away from the evening," he said, leaning in. I moved away, avoiding the kiss, his lips instead gracing my neck. A sly smile appeared on his face as if he had just accepted a challenge. I wasn't immediately attracted to Erik, but he projected a confidence that was appealing.

"Come on, lover boy. Let's make sure we didn't lose our reservation," I said, taking his arm and leading him up the stairs to the hostess station.

"Two for 6:30. Erik Becker," he announced like the president had just arrived. "That's a beautiful shirt. It really brings out your eyes," he said to the young hostess.

The girl blushed and smiled. "Thank you. We're really busy. I don't think we have anything open at the moment."

"I know we're late. It's all my fault. You see, I was so excited that this gorgeous woman agreed to go on a date with me and I got kind of nervous, so I decided to have a pre-date drink to take the edge off. You know how that is, right?"

The girl nodded, looking shyly down at the floor like she was being held captive, and in a way she was because she was stuck behind the podium with no escape route.

"Well," Erik continued with his obtrusive behavior, "I spilled the drink on my shirt, and of course I couldn't show up to a first date with the famous author, Dana Buckmir. By the way, have you heard of her? If you haven't, you should. She wrote this amazing book about her online dating experience. You have to order it on Amazon. Anyway, I digress. You see, I had to find another shirt and iron it. You know the rest. Please tell me you have something for us. I can't disappoint her after already keeping her waiting."

"I'm sure we can accommodate you, sir." She looked at the computer screen and then down at her book. She took two menus from the stack and instructed us to follow her.

"After you," he said, motioning for me to walk ahead of him. I whispered in his ear, "I think she just gave you what you wanted to get rid of you."

"I tend to get what I want," he said.

She led us to a table near the water's edge with a beautiful view of the marina. "Is this okay?" she asked.

"Perfect," Erik said.

We sat down. The hostess handed us menus. "Enjoy your dinner," she said before walking away.

Settled into our seats, there were a few seconds of silence. Erik stared at me a little too long and blurted out, "we'd make beautiful children."

"What?" My eyes widened.

"I'm sorry. Did I say that out loud? I was thinking it, but didn't realize I actually said it."

"You did, but I'll pretend you didn't," I said with a half-smile.

"I didn't mean it in a weird way. I was just admiring how beautiful you are and the thought came to mind."

"That's a first. I've never had someone say that to me within ten minutes of meeting. As a matter of fact, I don't think anyone has said that to me ever." Changing the subject, I said, "So is the story true that you were telling the hostess? You don't strike me as the type that gets nervous."

"Very perceptive, Ms. Buckmir. You're right. I don't generally get nervous, but I did have a wardrobe issue. I thought she'd take pity on me if I included the part with the nerves. You know, it added to the story."

"Would you consider yourself a storyteller?" I asked.

"As you say, we're all storytellers."

"Touché," I said.

Erik had done his research. He was quoting one of my Facebook posts.

He looked over the menu. "Let's order a drink. Shall we?"

"Good idea."

"Do you like margaritas?"

"I do."

"Oh, daaaling. No need to propose on the first date. Why don't you let me woo you a bit first?"

I laughed. "Well, since we're already having children, it just makes sense for us to get married," I said, going along with the banter. "How about those margaritas?"

The server came to the table. "Can I start you off with something to drink?"

"I'd like a margarita on the rocks with salt," I said.

"And for you sir?"

"Do you have a spicy margarita?"

"No, I'm sorry we don't. I can make it spicy though. I'll ask the bartender."

A few minutes later our drinks arrived. We held up our margaritas and clinked glasses. "Cheers." I took a sip of the sour drink. Erik took a sip of his, but winced.

"What's wrong?" I asked.

"I think the bartender just poured the bottle of tabasco in it."

"You asked for something spicy," I said. I waited for Erik's reaction to inform me more about his character. The first date was all about evaluating chemistry, as well as unveiling personality and values. Restaurants were the ideal environment for observing behaviors. Was he rude to the staff? Did he chew with his mouth open? Did he take the last bite of our shared appetizer?

"I guess I did, didn't I." Erik shrugged

The server returned. "How are your drinks?"

"I hate to bother you, chief, but this is a little too spicy. Do you mind bringing me a regular margarita?"

"Of course. I noticed the bartender putting the tabasco in, and didn't think it would be a hit. I'll take that off the bill and bring you our traditional margarita. I'm sorry about that."

"Not at all, boss. It was worth a try." He handed the drink back to him. "Thank you." Erik turned to me. "Sometime soon, I'll make you the best margarita ever. It's my signature drink."

I smiled and nodded. I liked how little things didn't bother him. Erik had a lightness about him that was magnetic. He was checking all of my boxes.

"So what do you do?" I asked.

"I recently left a twenty-year career in finance. I just felt myself burning out. I decided that I wanted to pursue my passion and open my own baking business. I'm going to call it Becker's Baked Goods."

"That's interesting. And the bartending job?"

"I thought it was important for me to have some experience in the restaurant business if I was going to start my own within the hospitality industry."

"That makes sense."

"I was a good boy and invested well, which gives me the financial freedom to pursue my passion."

"That's great," I said.

"You know what they say, 'love what you do, never work a day in your life.'"

It was clear Erik wanted to impress me with his eclectic palate and ability to expertly navigate a menu. He casually ordered without asking for my input. "Let's start with the octopus and a dozen oysters." The wind blew through his hair. He brushed it to one side and smiled.

"Enough about me, let's talk about you," he said. "Publishing a book is really quite an accomplishment. Your book is so funny and relevant. I really enjoyed it. I'm not much of a reader, but I was really captivated by your writing."

"Thank you." I blushed from his praise.

"I mean it. You should be proud," he continued with the adoration.

Anyone who says they don't like attention has never met Erik Becker. I was falling hard for his charm. Afterall, I was an English major. I loved words. And Erik's silver tongue knew exactly how to string words together to weave a quilt made of compliments that I was eager to embrace.

"There are six words I want to tell you," he said.

"Is that right?" I replied, intrigued by this creature sitting across from me who wielded words with such bravado.

"You know Dana, we've been going out for a while. You've met my parents and I've met yours."

My eyebrows raised at this statement. I laughed uncontrollably at Erik's ability to make fiction believable. The scene was set. The spotlight was on him. I had a front row seat to the show. It was one of those exchanges that was so ridiculous, I had to laugh at the absurdity of it.

He scratched the scruff on his chin and continued. "I need to say this. It's taken me a while to get the courage to say this." The intensity of his words were comparable to a method actor.

"Just go ahead and say it already," I said, getting swept away by his madness.

"I don't know any other way than just to blurt it out. I know you've been waiting a long time to hear six words from me."

"Right," I said pensively, wondering what kind of person could invent so effortlessly.

Erik drew out every word slowly, "Dana…I…love…you… so…much." Each word dripped off his lips like honey coated venom, sweet but deadly. *How could he look me in the eye and tell me he loved me when we had just met less than an hour ago?* The scary part of it was that he executed each word with precision, hypnotically lulling me under his spell. What frightened me even more was that I wanted to believe it was true.

"That's not what you're supposed to say," I said, laughing as a result of the mixture of margaritas and giddiness.

"That's six words, right?" he said.

I nodded and giggled.

"In all seriousness, I want to tell you something honestly."

He leaned closer for climactic effect. I thought about how my mother warned me to pay attention to people that announced they were being honest. Most likely, they were not. I don't think Erik was the exception.

"When I first discovered you online, I was compelled to send you a message."

Oh God, Lauren said I would receive a message.

He slicked his hair to the side again, taming it from the wind coming off the water. "Really, Dana, I usually don't extend myself. Generally, I look at a pretty girl online and think about needs versus wants. Of course, I want to message her, but with you I needed to. There was something different about you. Something special, and I knew that I'd regret it if I passed up the opportunity." He raised his finger and shook it at me with conviction, emphasizing his point.

"Wowwwwahhh," I said, taking his words in.

"When I did, I discovered how brilliantly funny you are, and just by surveying your Facebook profile, your videos, your comments, your posts… oh, and of course I read your book, which I do want signed, by the way." He pointed at me and glanced to the right, searching.

"So all kidding aside, Erik. What are the six words that you want to tell me?" I asked.

"Oh, right. That. I'm sorry I digressed. The six words that I want to tell you are, 'Dana you're the funniest person I've ever met.'"

I counted each word on my fingers until I got to eight. He shrugged and took a long sip from his margarita, draining the liquid down to the ice cubes.

"Bravo Erik, that was very interesting." I clapped for his Academy Award winning performance.

"Thank you very much. Please tip your bartender and try the meatloaf special." He reached his arm in the air and used his finger to make a circular motion indicating to the server to bring another round.

Our appetizers and drinks arrived. "Would you like to order your entrees?"

Erik plucked an oyster carefully, preparing it with horse-radish, cocktail sauce and a drop of vinegar, while the server waited patiently despite a full seating area.

"For you daaaling," he said, handing the oyster to me. He wiped his hands on the napkin and placed it back on his lap. He skimmed over the menu quickly. "Give me the biggest lobster you have."

"That's five pounds, sir." The server waited for confirmation.

"Fantastic. Hey boss, why don't you bring us a couple lobster rolls too."

"Anything else?" the server asked.

"That's all for now," he said. The tequila had heightened his personality.

After the server left the table I said, "Erik, are you sure about your order? That's a lot."

"Of course, daaaling. Only the best for you."

———∞———

The colorful hues of red, orange and purple cascaded across the sky, unveiling the upcoming sunset. I admired the ephemeral beauty, wanting to capture the moment.

"Have you ever seen the commercial with the guy that complains about his instagram girlfriend always making him take a million pictures of her for social media?" I asked.

"Yes I have, actually."

"Do you mind if we do it for a post?"

"Not at all," he said. Erik was amenable to my request.

I handed him my phone and he instructed me on how to pose. "Brush your hair away from your shoulder. Yes, that's it. Move to the left. Tilt your head to the side. Perfect."

I connected both index fingers and thumbs to meet, making a heart shape. Erik took the picture with the sunset in the background. I clicked on the Facebook app, uploaded the picture and captioned it with the hashtag, "Sunset heart hands."

After looking at the water, I turned back to Erik and said, "I absolutely love boats."

"My father has a boat," he said.

"Oh yeah. You should invite me on it sometime."

"Sure. You want to meet my parents already?" he asked.

"Well if we're having children, I think it makes sense for me to meet them, don't you?" I said teasing.

Looking at him with his button-down linen shirt, salmon shorts and boat shoes, he reminded me of the man that Carly Simon described in her song, *You're So Vain.*

"That's you," I said, humming the tune and singing the lyrics about a man walking into the party like he was walking onto a yacht.

He continued singing the next set of lyrics aloud. We took turns until we came to the chorus and belted out "you're so vain" so loud that the tables near us smiled and applauded.

"Thank you very much, good people," he said standing up to address the crowd as if he was the headliner of a show. "I'll be here all week. Well not here, but in the area. Encore upon request." He bowed and returned to his seat.

"You have a great voice." I told him. "I saw your karaoke videos online. Very impressive."

"Thank you, daaaling. Music is a big part of my life. I feel it in my soul."

"Haha, are you talking in an accent or is that your real voice?" I asked.

"I'm not sure what you mean, daaaling."

"Well, it's just that you seem like you're in character. I wonder what version of you I'll get next.

"I do have a knack for accents," he said, running his hair and tossing it in the wind like he was in a Pantene commercial, pleading with potential customers to not hate him because he was beautiful.

"I think you missed your calling as an actor. You said you had a finance career, right? There's always time to pursue acting. You have raw talent."

"Thank you, daaaling." We laughed some more. "When I was in finance, I remember sitting in a conference and the presenter was talking about finding your passion. Something hit me inside, and I realized that I wasn't where I needed to be. Yeah, it was good money, but it didn't bring me joy. I decided to leave and find something that did. Now, I just try to have fun and enjoy life."

We talked, but most of all, we laughed. There was no lull. No awkward silence that was typical of first dates, especially blind dates. The conversation flowed. It turned into an over three-hour date. We talked about my book and he shared about his experience on dating apps. Our exchange was playful. There was an immediate chemistry, sharing stories with a comfortability like we had known each other for years. *Could this be the guy that Lauren had said I would meet and fall in love with?*

The bill came to a little over three hundred dollars. He quickly grabbed it before I could offer, pulled out his card and said, "I'll get this."

I thanked him for his generosity. He walked me out to my car, opened my door, and wanted a proper first date kiss like the one he had proposed earlier. Instead, I gave him a peck on the cheek, to which he smiled as if I had passed a test. He closed the car door and waited until I was safely inside.

I started the car and rolled down the window. "I had a great time. Thank you for the perfect evening."

"It was the best first date ever," he said. He waved as I drove off.

And it really was the best first date ever. I hadn't laughed so much on a first date or been so entertained. Maybe this was my second chance at love. I was hooked and wanted more.

CHAPTER 4

After the best first date ever, I was excited to spend more time getting to know Erik. Our plan was to go to the beach. He would meet at my house at nine the next morning. I thought something was wrong when he didn't show and I didn't hear from him. I immediately panicked, letting insecurity take over. *Was I ghosted?* Maybe the date hadn't gone as well as I thought. Maybe he didn't share the same feelings. I texted him. No response. My anxiety grew when I called his phone and went straight to voicemail.

Finally, a few hours later, I got a text from him.

On a scale of 1-10, how pissed are you?

I resisted the urge to text back immediately, not wanting to seem desperate. After a sufficient amount of time, I replied.

No words

At least I knew he wasn't dead. When I didn't pick up the phone, he sent me a long voice message.

"I want to sincerely apologize for this morning. I went to start up my Jeep. I got about a mile down the road; it started stalling and conked out and the engine went off. I was pissed because I had the car serviced yesterday. I told the mechanic about the stalling. It ended up being a faulty spark plug loose connection. Now it's working fine. I was a little perturbed about that. When I went over to the mechanic, my phone was dead and he didn't have an iPhone charger, only a Samsung, so of course I would have called you, but I couldn't. He said it would only take like fifteen minutes to figure it out and ended up taking a lot longer. Again, I want to apologize. You must be thinking 'oh my god, this guy doesn't give a shit,' and I'm probably acting like all the other assholes that you've met, and I just want to let you know that I'm not the typical asshole that you've met. I am different and I am sincere and I do care about time management and I'm very disappointed in myself for this morning. I just want to let you know that. And when you said 'no words,' I was like, great, she went into silent mode, which means she's really pissed off. I don't blame you. I just want to apologize, and shoot me a text, reach out to me if you want to reschedule. I hope you're doing alright and you're not too mad. Sorry. Sorry. Sorryyyyyy. Bye. Kiss Kiss."

Something about all the details in his apology made me question the validity of his message. From our first date, he had shown he was an elaborate storyteller. But why go through the long explanation if it wasn't meaningful? Afterall, we had only gone on one date. He didn't owe me anything. Was I being too skeptical? Had I been burnt so many times that I was letting the wreckage of my previous disaster relationships seep into this one? The apology seemed heartfelt, so why did I get an uneasy feeling? He said he was sincere. He said he was disappointed in himself, but was he really? There was something about him and the writer in me that felt compelled to explore the relationship, even if I knew it would take me to places I didn't want to go.

Mia had scolded me on our phone call for not looking into Erik.

"How can you have written a book about dating and you've never looked anyone up on the judicial website?"

"Is that really a thing that people do?" I asked.

"Um, yeah! You of all people should know there are a ton of crazies out there. You can never be too careful. Do yourself a favor and look him up."

"I'll think about it," I said.

My conversation with Mia had made me curious. Maybe I should look him up. I opened up my laptop to the search engine and typed in "State of Connecticut Judicial Look Up."

It brought me to the main home page. I clicked on convicted cases and typed in his first and last name and pressed submit.

A case appeared from 2016 between Erik and a Nina Becker. It was a violation of a protective order. *And this is exactly why I don't look people up. What am I supposed to do with this information?*

I messaged Erik back.

> *Thanks for the heartfelt apology.*
> *Let's meet at the dog park.*

Yes, meet you there in 20 minutes.
I promise I won't let you down.

Dogs frolicked in the open area. Some chased balls. Others chased each other. My dog, Lucky, sniffed the trees while I followed closely behind him. Erik walked across the park wearing a Pink Floyd shirt and an apologetic look on his face. This time he wasn't late. He slicked his hair to the side and smiled widely. His eyes shimmered in the afternoon sunlight. Before he apologized, I had already forgiven him.

"Thanks for seeing me again," he said.

"Everyone deserves a second chance," I said.

We walked around the park. Enjoying the weather. Talking casually. Until finally I couldn't help myself. I had to say something about what I discovered on the judicial website.

"So I was looking you up today and I saw a conviction listed from 2016."

Erik's smile faded and was replaced with a furrowed brow. Panic took over his expression.

"I can explain," he said. "The woman is my wife – I mean, my ex-wife, Nina," he said, clarifying.

"I didn't know you had an ex-wife," I said.

"I was going to tell you, but I just didn't think it was something I should share on the first date."

"Okay," I said, waiting for him to continue.

"You see she's a very troubled woman. She has a major issue with alcohol. I've tried tirelessly to help her, but nothing worked. On occasions she became violent. This was one of those times. I was working in the city at a finance job. I had just gotten home, and she was already drunk. She was rambling about something. I was exhausted. I just wanted my space. I went to lie down in the bedroom after a long day. She followed behind me and mounted me on the bed. I could smell the alcohol on her breath. I asked her to get off of me. She refused. When I went to push her off, she fell to the ground and hit her head. She became angry and blamed me. Then she called the police on me. I was arrested. She stuck to her story. I went back to the house because all of my belongings were there and I needed them for work. When I arrived at our house she called the police, which was considered a violation of the protective order."

"Wow, that's crazy," I said. "I'm sorry you had to deal with that. That must have been hard."

"It was. You have no idea how difficult it is to love someone who struggles with addiction and mental illness. They act irrationally. Not only do they hurt themselves, but the people around them who have to watch helplessly as they spiral out of control. My only regret is that I couldn't do more to help her."

I gave him a hug. Moisture filled his eyes. It looked like talking about the past had reopened old wounds that made him emotional. I felt bad for him.

"Thank you for being understanding," he said. "I was worried that you wouldn't talk to me after this."

"Everyone has a past. I appreciate you explaining yours to me."

We walked hand-in-hand around the park. I felt close to him. He had disclosed something painful from his past. He didn't have to tell me. Choosing to do so showed me that he was being honest and wanted to share a part of himself with me.

CHAPTER 5

I hadn't talked to Mia since my first date with Erik. She messaged me to follow up.

Hey girl. Just got up and heard your voicemail.
Glad you had an amazing date the other night.
I'm your maid of honor when you get married.

He violated a restraining order

Red flag city!

I asked him about it

Do you feel better now?

I think so.

Important question?

Shoot!

Do I… A) Go have a frozen margarita.
B) Go to the pool. C) Do Laundry. D) Read a book.

> *I love it when you do the*
> *multiple choice. A & B for the*
> *win. I wish you lived closer.*
> *I'd do A & B with you every*
> *day.*

Erik arrived at my house carrying a paper bag filled with groceries. I was instructed not to look inside, since it was a surprise.

Having Erik make me dinner in my father's kitchen brought back memories of him. I learned at a young age that men made great chefs. My father was a printer by trade and a chef by heart. He had no formal training. In fact, I don't even think he graduated from high school. Watching him cook was my first glimpse into witnessing the satisfaction a person received by preparing a meal. He never measured anything. A pinch of this. A handful of that.

"Sharing your craft is like exposing a part of your soul," he had said. Only when I was older did I fully understand what he meant. His craft was the culinary arts, while mine was the written word. Both of us were seeking a connection between the creator and the consumer. I wasn't allowed to participate in the ritual. He was very territorial over his kitchen. It was a sacred space. One that brought him great happiness. I could stand in the doorway and watch with the understanding that I was quiet and didn't ask any questions. "You don't mess with a masterpiece," he had said.

As a quiet observer, I studied my father: the focus and control he had when creating a dish. The time and effort he took using only the best ingredients. My father made magic in the kitchen. Growing up, I don't remember him ever telling me that he loved me. But from the meals he created, I knew he did. Food was love.

Erik had a similar sense of pride in the kitchen. His smile lit up his face while he laid out all of the ingredients on the counter. I found myself returning to the quiet observer in the doorway as Erik chopped the onions and the garlic. The aroma filled up the room as he sauteed them in olive oil.

"I'm going to make you the best dinner ever," he proclaimed in a thick British accent that was reminiscent of Robin Leach from *Lifestyles of the Rich and Famous*.

Everything to him was about being the best. The best lover. The best boyfriend who baked the best cheesecake. The best host who mixed the best margaritas.

One time I asked him, "why do you try so hard to be the best?" It was probably one of the only times he was ever honest with me.

He said, "if I'm the best, you won't leave me," with a sadness in his voice like he had experienced a lifetime of loss.

He took out a bottle of wine.

"Where is the wine key?" he asked casually, opening the drawers around him.

"Next to the stove," I said, pointing in the direction of the kitchen.

He uncorked the bottle and poured a glass, handing me the Malbec, my favorite. Erik paid attention to what I liked. He was a quick study. After pouring his own glass, he held his to mine, clinked them together and said, looking at me intently, "cheers to you, gorgeous. Go relax outside. I'll let you know when dinner's ready."

I took a sip of wine. As the flavors warmed my mouth, I couldn't help but feel a sense of gratitude for Erik. I had been a person who was used to taking care of others. It felt good to have someone else take care of me. I went along with his take-charge attitude, because it wasn't every day that a man brought groceries to my house and offered to cook dinner.

My phone buzzed. It was Mia checking on our date.

Soooooo??

> *He's cooking dinner.*

Ahhhh, I want someone to cook me dinner.
I'd settle for someone to bring me tacos
and leave.

> *It sounds like you need*
> *UberEats.*

Give me the deets.

> *He's spectacular.*

Dana, I'm so happy for you.

DANA BUCKMIR

You deserve it!

> *It's been a long time. I'm going to savor every moment.*

He called me inside as a parent does, "Dinneeerrrr."

> *Dinner's ready. Gotta go.*
> *TTYL*

Mangia momma, mwah.

Dinner turned out to be exactly what I wanted, linguine Fra Diablo with calamari.

"This is really delicious, Erik. Thank you," I said, twirling the linguine to form a tightly rolled package of pasta..

"My pleasure." A sense of accomplishment gleamed across his face.

Erik knew I loved Italian food. He said he saw it on my Facebook page, although I don't remember posting about it. If he said so, he must have been right. It was probably a while ago.

We sat in the kitchen, dining over candlelight. "Alexa dinner playlist." Moments later a Fleetwood Mac song streamed through the speaker, the lead vocalist singing about being under a spell. I could relate, because there was something enchanting about Erik that made me feel like time stopped when we were in each other's company. It was like he knew me, and we had just met. *How could I feel such a strong connection in a short time?* Perhaps the wine was going to my head.

"You made your own date night dinner compilation?"

50

He nodded his head in between bites of seafood. "Only the best for you, daaaling," he said.

He poured some more wine in each glass. Raising his in the air, "I propose a toast to more dinners with you, beautiful, smart, witty, ambitious Dana Buckmir. I hope that one day you can understand how truly honored I am to be in your company," he said like he was giving a speech in a crowded room of benefactors, readily waiting to open their wallets to contribute to whatever cause he deemed worthy. There was something rehearsed and disingenuous about his rhetoric, as if he were a D-list actor reading from a teleprompter. But I ignored the feeling, attributing it to his theatrical personality. Who was I to question a man who insisted on treating me like a princess? I needed this. I deserved this.

"Finish up. I have another surprise for you after dinner," he said, smiling pleasantly.

Full of pasta and flushed with wine, I cleared the table. Erik went outside for a cigarette and to retrieve my other surprise from his Jeep. I scraped the leftover sauce into the garbage and stacked the plates in the sink, running the hot water over them.

Lucky ran to the door, barking, announcing Erik's return.

"Take a seat and close your eyes," he instructed.

I listened obediently, covering my eyes with my hands.

"What are you up to, Erik Becker?"

"Oh, you'll see," he said.

Seconds later he announced that I could open my eyes. He presented me with a small box, placing it in my hands.

Inside was a keychain with "you are my sunshine" inscribed in a sunflower.

"Oh, Erik. Thank you. This is so sweet."

"One more surprise," he said, reaching behind him for a bag. "Ta daaaa!"

Inside the bag were toys and treats for Lucky.

"You're so thoughtful. Thank you so much," I said.

I was truly enamored with this man. It had been a long time since someone spoiled me, and I was enjoying every moment.

CHAPTER 6

Erik had left early before I awoke. As part of my morning routine, I put on a pot of coffee before taking Lucky outside. The machine percolated, dripping through to the carafe, filling the kitchen with a coffee aroma that I needed after a late night. Erik and I had stayed up until after midnight, talking. It was refreshing to have someone to share my life with. Someone who listened. Someone who cared. Someone who wanted to know every detail.

I opened up my laptop preparing to write, like I did every morning. I needed to have something ready to share with my weekly writing group. As my mentor had reminded me, "the book isn't going to write itself."

Lucky scratched on the door, gesturing that he couldn't wait to do his business. And so, begrudgingly, I took him outside, leaving the coffee and my work in progress behind. After he finished, I pulled him towards the door, looking forward to diving into the next chapter and taking the first sip of coffee that waited inside. I turned the door knob, but it wouldn't open. It was locked. *No, that couldn't be.* I tried again, but it didn't budge. I realized that Erik had locked the bottom lock and didn't tell me.

Are you kidding me?

I panicked. How was I going to get back in the house? My heart started racing as I ran around the house, checking if all of the windows and doors were locked. There was no use. I was locked out. My phone was sitting inside where I had left it on the kitchen counter. To add insult to injury, I was barely dressed, wearing only a t-shirt, no bra, flip flops and boxers. This was definitely not how I envisioned starting the morning. I thought of the best way to get back in that would cause the least amount of damage. I tied Lucky to the lead outside and looked around the yard for something to use to break the window. I decided that the only way in was through the bathroom window. I found a rock and pulled a lawn chair over to use as a step. Balancing on the chair, I hurled the rock into the glass. Surprisingly, it broke on the first try. I used the same rock to chip away at the edges of the window frame. I picked off the large pieces, clearing an entry way big enough for me to hoist myself through. I pressed up and heaved my body through the opening.

When I got back in the house, I took an assessment of the damage and snapped a picture to send it to Erik.

Not exactly how I expected to start my morning.

Whaaaat happened?

Um, you locked me out.

Omg, I'm really sorry about that. Window will be repaired.

Thank you.

It's the least I can do.

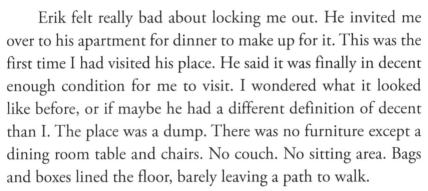

Erik felt really bad about locking me out. He invited me over to his apartment for dinner to make up for it. This was the first time I had visited his place. He said it was finally in decent enough condition for me to visit. I wondered what it looked like before, or if maybe he had a different definition of decent than I. The place was a dump. There was no furniture except a dining room table and chairs. No couch. No sitting area. Bags and boxes lined the floor, barely leaving a path to walk.

"Did you just move in?" I asked.

"No, I've been here since January."

It was August.

"The place isn't normally like this, but my roommate, Britney, just moved out. These are her things," he said, looking around at the mess.

I walked around, inspecting the space as he prepared a meat and cheese board. Britney's clothes were left behind, thrown on the floor. Her undergarments poured out of one of the bags. It looked like she left in a hurry.

We sat outside. The night breeze made me forget about the inside of the apartment. We sipped champagne under a star-filled sky.

"If I get you addicted to my cooking, you won't leave me." Erik said. He laughed.

I smiled and took a bite of the chicken, the rich sauce combined with the tender meat melted in my mouth.

At the time I thought his comment was endearing, but looking back now, it revealed a lot about his abandonment issues and alluded to the fact that people didn't stay in his life for too long.

I couldn't help but be hypnotized by this man that wanted nothing more than to please me. It had been a while since I had felt like this. I didn't want to lose it. At that moment, I was mesmerized by him. The glow on his face from the candlelight. The sparks between us.

He held his glass up. "I'd like to make a toast to my soulmate, my end game. You're everything I've ever dreamed of. Everything I've ever wanted. I'm going to make you the happiest woman alive," he said.

"Cheers." We clinked our glasses together.

I held the glass to my lips and took a sip.

I wanted to believe it. What woman wouldn't want to be showered with praise and promised a lifetime of love and happiness? I devoured his words as if they were the sustenance I needed to survive. I thought that after everything I had endured, this was finally my chance to have it all. Why couldn't I have everything? I deserved it. I was worth it. This was my chance at a happy ending.

I felt as if I had hit the jackpot. My prayers had finally been answered. I had met a decent man with all the qualities I could ask for. Kind. Loving. Generous. Thoughtful. Funny. Intelligent. Handsome. And the best part: he was all mine.

I had been waiting for it all my life, and finally it was within reach. The universe had given me a gift. I had no idea how far from the truth that was.

"Do you do this for all the girls?" I asked slyly.

"My father once said that if you want a woman to come back, you have to give her something she's never had before."

For dessert, he fed me gelato. "The thing that makes gelato so appealing," he said, "is that even after you've swallowed it, the essence still lingers on your tongue."

I was smitten. I wanted him to be my last bite. To linger on my tongue. To taste him.

That night, he played guitar and sang about lying me down in a bed of roses. I felt the emotion in his voice as the words moved sweetly from his lips. Many women would have loved for a man like Erik to cook a candlelit dinner and serenade them. I was special. He had chosen me. I was the lucky one.

He grabbed my face and pulled me in, kissing me softly.

He paused for a moment. "Are you okay with this?"

"Yes. Yes!" I said, thinking no one had ever asked my consent before. It felt so foreign. It was such a simple question, one that should have been asked, yet no one before Erik had ever bothered to get permission to make sure I was okay.

That night we made love. He touched me gently. Heat radiating between us. We ebbed and flowed like waves. A spectacular synergy of two bodies becoming one. Afterwards, he held me close. His arms wrapped around my body. Protective in his embrace.

"Do I make you feel safe?" he asked.

"Yes," I answered.

In that moment, the world outside faded. There was no him or me. Only us. Our bodies tangled up amongst crumpled sheets. Our souls united. He stroked my hair. He kissed me on the forehead. Tickling my skin, he grazed his fingers up and down my arm, sending tingles throughout. The only sound in the room was of our hearts beating and the soothing sound of his voice whispering softly to me.

"You're my home. I want this to last forever."

"Me too," I said, a single tear rolling down my face. *Me too.*

"It's simple. Love me and I'll love you. We'll love each other as we are and as we should," he said.

I got lost in his words. *Did he just tell me he loved me?* It was too soon to be in love. Or was it?

"Don't you think it's too soon to use the L-word?" I asked.

He put his hand on my mouth signaling me to stop speaking in the process, silencing my worries. He removed his hand and replaced it with his mouth. His warm, wet tongue pushed inside. He pinned my arms up above my head and kissed me fiercely biting my lip.

He scooped me up in his arms. My legs wrapped around his body and I melted into him. Our bodies molded together perfectly.

"We fit together," he whispered in my ear.

I closed my eyes and exhaled. Even if we didn't, I wanted to believe that we did. Isn't that what everyone wanted? To try and find the one missing piece that makes us whole. It could be love or the endorphins, but Erik seemed like a good prospect.

Maybe when you meet the right person, everything aligns and you just know. It's something that can't be explained. It's a feeling. This was my chance at happiness. In the past, I may have acted like I didn't want this, but underneath the tough exterior was a little girl that grew up watching the same romantic comedies, rooting for the girl to get the guy. Of course I wanted a happy ending.

"I've been waiting twenty years to fall in love. You're my soulmate." He kissed me like he was kissing me for the last time. Lingering. Holding me tight so I wouldn't slip away. I wanted to hold onto him and never let him go.

It sounded like something out of a fairytale, and I wanted to believe so badly that it was real. That I could get the story book ending.

Within minutes he was asleep. His chest rose and fell. His rhythmic breathing like a quiet growl rumbling lulled me to a peaceful state. He turned over. I traced the beauty marks on his back with my finger, following the curves, connecting the dots like a constellation of clusters. I could read his body like a map, navigating me towards my destiny.

CHAPTER 7

*H*ow *was your sex date?* Mia didn't hold back.
I texted back immediately, eager to share the magic I had experienced.

Amazing!

Aww, I'm so happy for you.

I love beginnings.

Yep, enjoy that honeymoon stage.

Oh, I will. What's going on with you?

Nothing much. Another hard day of hanging out by the pool and maybe a frozen margarita.

Life is good.

I thought that writing the first book was hard, but the second was just as challenging, maybe even more. Writer's block was real. The weekly writing group gave me the motivation that I needed. Only problem was that I didn't feel like I had a story to share. Everyone came with a piece to read. The facilitator, Mary, took turns going around the room. Each writer read their excerpt and the others provided written and verbal feedback.

Diedre had the worst story. It was a gruesome one that made me cringe and want to unhear what I couldn't. I purposely sat far away from her when we'd meet in our weekly writing sessions, as if what she read was contagious. Maybe if I physically distanced myself from her, I could prevent what she had from getting on me. We met in the church basement while the library was being renovated. The AA meeting that ended before ours left the chairs in a circle. We didn't feel the need to move them.

We sat on the cold, hard collapsible chairs, our bodies and souls exposed to each other. Stale coffee, powder creamer and a stack of Styrofoam cups lay on the table next to the bibles. A faint scent of cigarettes lingered in the air. I always wondered what God would say if he heard the stories that echoed from the walls.

Diedre was broken from living a life sentence of abuse. It was her turn to share this week, and I dreaded hearing her read. She walked with a cane, partly from age and partly from what he did to her. A fake eye was a reminder of the time he took a crowbar to her face. She sat solemnly. Her shaking hands holding up a piece of notebook paper with illegible scribbles. She squinted and read softly, the volume so faint we had to strain to hear her. Nobody would dare ask her to speak up.

"I always had anxiety around the same time every night, because that was the time that Claude was expected to come home." Her pointer finger moved across the page as she read aloud. "It was quarter to seven and he would be home soon. He wanted dinner exactly as he demanded, and if he didn't get it, I was in trouble. I prepared the fried chicken as I always did. A side of homemade macaroni and cheese and some collard greens finished out the dish. The hinge on the door needed to be oiled and the creek, when he opened it, sounded like something out of a horror movie. I smelled him before I saw him. The mix of sweat and liquor announced his arrival."

Diedre continued to depict what we already knew. Claude found something wrong with his dinner, and Diedre's body and spirit paid the price.

Mary listened intently to Diedre's story. A single tear rolled down her face when Diedre described the details of the assault. "You're such an inspiration, Diedre. You being here today and sharing your story with us is a testament to your strength. God will bless you and watch over you as you continue with your healing process."

Mary organized the writing group. She was an optimist and could find the best in any situation. We needed more Marys in this world to balance out the Claudes. Listening to Diedre's story made me realize how so many monsters masqueraded as humans.

Something made me uneasy about Diedre's story. She was an amazing writer and a pillar of strength. No one would argue that her writing wasn't powerful. I'm not sure I'd be able to survive what she had. I couldn't help but think that I could never be Deidre. How did she allow this man to beat her down physically and emotionally day after day? I felt removed from her story like I couldn't identify. I pitied her and felt awful for not recognizing the courage this woman possessed. I hate to admit it, but I took comfort in knowing that her story would never be mine. Never. Those kinds of things happened to people like Diedre. Not me.

I left the group feeling dejected, but relieved to escape and get some air. I sent Mia a text.

How's your day going?

Can't complain. You?

I just had a seriously depressing writing group session.

Why?

A woman wrote about her domestic violence situation. Total bummer.

That's heavy

Yeah, I think I'll take a little time off from the group. I can't relate.

*I get it. You're on cloud nine all
caught up in being love drunk in
the land of unicorns and rainbows.*

Right!

*Take some time off if it's not helping. You can
always go back another time when you feel up to it.*

True.

I dug my feet in the sand. A light breeze coming off the water rustled my hair. The sun beamed down, filling my face with warmth. Summer was fleeting. I was determined to enjoy every minute of beach time before it was gone. And in New England, that was all too fast.

Erik sat in a chair holding my book. He flipped through the pages, reading aloud the experiences of my life. Each character was given a different voice, making it more theatrical. His voice was rich and vibrant, projecting each scene with passion like he was performing on stage. I grew to discover that everything with Erik was a performance. It was hard to distinguish what was genuine and what was acting. We laughed. I commented that he should have been an actor, as I did on our first date, never thinking that he actually was. In between chapters, he remarked how intrigued he was by my experiences and asked questions to learn more. I smiled blissfully. It felt good to have someone take an interest in my writing.

It had been a while since I had felt appreciated. In retrospect, I was probably a little too hungry for it, which made me ignore the warning signs. The questions weren't natural. They were intrusive like he was testing the boundaries and deep diving for secrets he could use later as ammunition. Erik praised me often, but he always found a way to incorporate some form of criticism.

"Let's take a selfie." He held his arm above us and snapped a picture. I watched him zoom in, examining my face.

"You know that when you smile, your right eye closes," he said.

"Really? I never noticed. Maybe I'm squinting from the sun," I said, shrugging the comment off. I turned my focus to the older couple walking along the beach, hand-in-hand. The man periodically stopped to pick up a shell and present it to the woman beside him.

"Take a look." He reached over and showed me his phone, pointing to my eye.

"Doesn't everyone's eye do that?" I asked.

"No. You have a lazy eye," he said as if he were an optometrist.

"A lazy eye? I don't think so." I shook my head in disagreement.

"It's charming, though. It's one of the things I love about you. Your imperfections make you beautiful and unique."

It didn't feel charming. It felt like I was being attacked. *Who says that to someone?* I thought. Even if it were true, it was rude to make a person feel self-conscious about their body, especially something they couldn't change.

Erik noticed I was quiet and playfully threw sand on the blanket near me to get my attention. "It's cute. Don't be so sensitive." He chuckled.

"I'm going swimming. Want to come?" I stood up from the blanket, wiping the sand off my body, and motioned for him to get up. He put the book down and followed, clasping my hand in his. He brushed the hair away from my face and kissed my right eye as if to prove his point even further that his comment wasn't a threat, but another form of admiration.

I couldn't help but wonder why he would think that his comment was appropriate. His body was far from perfect, but I would never think to say anything about it. If anyone else had said that to me, it would be grounds for an argument, yet Erik had a way to package a criticism in the form of a compliment, wrapping up the insult with a beautiful bow. And if I became offended, it was just a joke. I should have a better sense of humor, after all. Although at the time, those interactions seemed harmless. Reflecting, I realize now that they were an opportunity for Erik to see what he could get away with, all the while exposing my vulnerabilities.

The tension dissipated with the water. We moved with the waves. I felt free. The water shimmered like crystals from the sun's reflection. The tide moved in and out with a melodic rhythm. Erik jabbered on about his business plan to make desserts and sell them to local bakeries. It was an entrepreneurial goal that he had started once before and sought to revisit. He told me a story about one coffee shop in particular that he had a solid partnership with until the owner's obsession with him changed the dynamic, and the relationship went south. Erik always had a story that followed the same formula. He met someone, things went well for a while, then some conflict arose, and the relationship tragically ended. Of course, he was always the innocent party, the victim of some injustice. This story, like the rest, just didn't sound right to me.

"Yeah, so she would talk to me about her divorce. I knew she was into me, and I wasn't interested. When I told her that I just wanted to keep our partnership professional, she lashed out and screamed at me. I knew then that it wasn't going to work out. Another scorned woman taking her emotional baggage out on me."

I focused on the waves, tuning out most of Erik's words. Then, mid-sentence, he stopped. "You see that woman over there, we used to work out together."

"Oh, okay," I said, not thinking much of it.

"Hey Irina," Erik called out to the heavily muscled Russian weightlifter.

She squinted, placing her hand up against her forehead, shielding her eyes from the sun. She was attempting to make recognition, and by her face I could tell she was able to place him. I wasn't surprised, considering Erik was a memorable character.

Erik waded over to the woman. "Irina, I want you to meet my girlfriend, my soulmate, my end game." He pulled me closer to him, squeezing me tightly like a snake with its prey.

We stood waist deep in the water. Erik went on about his business that was at this point just an idea, but he made it sound like it was a successful enterprise. Irina nodded. She was hard to read, so I couldn't tell if she detected his bullshit.

I tried not to engage, already put off by Erik's over the top professions of love for me.

"Irina, tell Dana how much fun we had with our crossfit group. I really need to get back in shape. As you can see, I'm a little soft," he said, grabbing his belly.

"You should definitely come back." Irina walked out of the water looking back. "Sorry, I gotta run. It was great seeing you, Erik. And nice meeting you, Dana."

I smiled and waved. "You too," Erik said.

After my date with Erik, I felt insecure and needed a second opinion, so I messaged Mia.

Do I have a lazy eye?

WTF! Who said that?

Erik

You have beautiful eyes, Dana.
Why would he say that?

I furiously typed taking my frustrations out on the keypad.

I have no idea. Rude, right?

Totally. Even if you did have a lazy eye,
I wouldn't tell you.

So I do?

No, you don't

But you wouldn't tell me.

Stop! She wrote with a stop sign emoji

CHAPTER 8

Beth was an emotionally unstable, violent drunk. At least that's how Erik described her. They dated for a little less than two years. He said he felt sorry for her because she had a hard time letting go of the relationship, so the nature of theirs was off and on. Their nights were fueled with intoxicated fights and obsessive jealousy. I had no reason not to believe him. I didn't know Beth. I did find it coincidental that he described his ex-wife the same way. She, too, was mentally unstable and suffered from drug and alcohol problems. If I thought back to all the conversations that Erik had with me about his exes, they all shared the same issue: drunk and crazy. Either Erik had horrible luck with relationships, or there was more to the story. At first, I thought that he was being open and forthcoming with his past. I never asked him about any of his relationships. *Why would he willingly offer information if he had something to hide?* I slowly started to realize that by telling his version before I heard it from someone else allowed him to frame the narrative. It was a calculated move.

We had only been dating for a month when Beth contacted me. I received a message request from her since we weren't friends on Facebook. I clicked on the folder and the name Beth Rosenfeld appeared under the People You May Know tab.

Dana, I'm warning you right now about Erik…

I could only see the first part of the message. I clicked on "Approve message" to read the rest.

Please be careful. He still has an open court case with not only me, but his wife and other women. You seem to be awesome. You don't need to be abused.

I didn't know how to respond. *Abused?* What was this woman talking about? Hearing Erik had open court cases with multiple women was a shock to say the least. The comment about me being awesome threw me off too. Erik had told me about her, but how did she know about me? And the clear labeling of him as an abuser was alarming. Not knowing what to say, I defaulted to a message that sounded more like an automated response than an actual person.

Hi Beth. Thanks for reaching out.

Love, I'm being serious.

Ugh. She called me Love. I couldn't stand when people used annoying pet names without even knowing the person. It felt condescending and fake, especially for someone that was my age. I wanted her to get to the point already.

What would you like to warn me about?

Can I trust you?

Could she trust me? That was a weird question. How could you trust someone you don't even know? I wanted her to trust me enough to talk to me, so I had to be delicate to avoid scaring her away.

I'd like to hear what you have to say.

He punched me too many times. I told my mother. She made me lose him, which I'm still not over.

Punched her? Too many times? I had to hear her story.

Call me.

After talking to Beth, I didn't know what to think. At that time, I hadn't seen any signs of abuse. He wasn't violent. He had never raised his voice or called me a name. I paid attention to things like how he reacted to alcohol to ensure that I wasn't getting involved with a guy that had issues when he drank. There were no red flags. In fact, I thought back on the few times that we disagreed, and there really was no conflict. We'd just laugh it off. But this girl seemed serious. I wouldn't even think about reaching out to one of my exes' new girlfriends. She must have felt strongly about it in order to contact me.

I wanted to believe her, but to be honest, she did sound a little unstable. We talked in the afternoon, and she was slurring her words and getting overly emotional. Maybe Erik was right about her. I heard her out, but now it was time for me to give Erik the courtesy of hearing his side. She was slinging some pretty serious allegations. I owed him the opportunity to explain. We had plans for him to come over that night, so I waited to talk to him in person.

The loud muffler announced his arrival. I sat waiting in the darkness. The night sky threw glints of light across his face as he emerged from the distance. His signature wind-blown "Jeep hair don't care" paired with the Fender t-shirt and cargo shorts was either a tribute to the grunge decade, or he was still wearing his old clothes from the 1990s.

"What are you doing sitting out here?" He looked at me strangely.

"I talked to Beth today." So much for small talk. I had waited long enough to confront him. Beth and I had finished our conversation this afternoon. I had been digesting the information for hours, acting like everything was normal when he messaged me. Telling him that I couldn't wait to see him. That was true. I couldn't wait to see him so I could ask him about everything she had told me. I wanted answers. I wanted to give him the opportunity to explain his side and see his reaction in person. I needed to read his expressions and body language, something that couldn't be observed via text.

"Why would you talk to her?" The carefree expression that was on his face had been replaced with irritation.

"She messaged me."

"And you didn't block her?" He took a seat next to me.

"I wanted to hear what she had to say."

"What lies did she tell you about me?"

"She warned me that you're abusive… that you hit her and other women." I struggled to say those words aloud.

"Oh, Dana. Do you really believe that? I told you about her. She's obsessed. The girl sits in her mother's basement and drinks every night."

I was surprised at how casually he registered being called an abuser. He was dismissive. You'd think that if he was accused of something of that magnitude, he'd have some reaction. Instead, he took another long drink from the can and rustled in his pocket for a pack of Camels. He lit one and sat back in the chair, seemingly unaffected.

"Why would she make that up, Erik?"

"Isn't it obvious? She wants to ruin what we have. I told you about her. She's a scorned woman who realizes that she messed up a good thing and now she's trying to prevent us from being happy. She's toxic, Dana." He reached over to grab my hand.

"She sounded concerned… and scared." I pulled my hand away. A shiver ran down my back.

"Come on. She's a good actress. You know me. Have I ever hit you? He leaned over, his elbows on his knees, looking me in the eye. His face filled with innocence, eyes looked kind and honest.

"No." I said, shaking my head. I shuddered at the thought of a man putting his hands on me in that way. *He couldn't pos-*

sibly be capable. I tried to convince myself that it wasn't true, all the while a feeling of overwhelming apprehension signaled something was wrong.

"She said that you punched her. Why would she say that? And she said that she had a court case with you. That is true. I looked it up."

"Baby, what you saw is her blowing the situation completely out of proportion. She was drunk, of course. I was driving, and she was accusing me of talking to other women. She was insanely jealous and insecure. She grabbed the wheel of the Jeep and almost caused an accident. I pushed her off of the wheel so she wouldn't kill us both. When I was able to pull the Jeep over and try to calm her down, she started punching me, and I grabbed her arms to defend myself. All I did was hold her and make her stop hitting me. She was completely out of control."

"It just… I don't know. It just doesn't make sense, Erik."

"I'll call her if you don't believe me, and you can see for yourself how unstable she is."

After finding her in his contacts, he hit the call button and put it on speaker so we both could hear.

She answered on the first ring, "Hi, Daddy Lion." A seductive tone in her voice and a comfort level revealed that they talked often.

My stomach turned.

"I heard you had a lot to say to my girlfriend this afternoon."

"Your girlfriend? She wasn't your girlfriend two weeks ago when you slept with me."

Ignoring her comment, he said, "Beth, why are you telling Dana lies? You know I never touched you."

"They're not lies. Can you come over, Daddy? Baby Kitten needs you."

I couldn't listen any longer. The bile had moved from my stomach, filling up my throat.

"Hi, Baby Kitten. It's Dana. You're on speaker."

"Ohhh. Erik, you put me on speaker? Why would you do that?"

Daddy Lion was now Erik.

"Because I want to know why you're spreading lies about me. Beth, you need to move on. I have."

"With that girl? She looks like a horse. She's not even pretty."

"Helllooooo. Did you get the memo that you're on speaker?" I said. Clearly she didn't care if I heard her insults. Beth wasn't winning any brownie points from me.

I sat and listened to the conversation unfold, not wanting to interrupt, but wanting to observe the dynamic between the two. She was quickly losing credibility, especially with the jabs to my appearance, the sad attempts to inflate her ego at my expense. She sounded exactly as Erik had described her – a jealous ex who couldn't let it go.

"Did you tell her how you punched me? How you dragged me by the hair across the kitchen floor?"

"Stop it, Beth. You need help. You sound drunk. You're slurring your words." He turned to me and gave an affirming nod, gesturing with his hands up to his mouth, indicating that she was inebriated. "I never touched you and you know that."

She cried. "How could you do this to me? All I ever did was love you. I still love you. You destroyed me."

She sounded pathetic. I felt sorry for her. She was obviously hurting, but listening to her now, it became clear that she hadn't gotten over him. I just couldn't understand that if Erik had abused her, why would she want to be with him? Obviously, if that happened she would have left him and never spoken to him again. *Who stayed with their abuser?* In one breath she was accusing him of violence. In another she was asking him to come over. It didn't make sense.

"I don't love you, Beth. Move on and stop spreading lies."

"They're not lies," she repeated. "I wanted to warn her so she didn't end up like me." Her voice trailed off in a defeated tone.

"I'll never be like you, Beth," I said, unable to restrain myself from jabbing back.

"You need help, and if you don't stop harassing my girlfriend, I'm going to get a restraining order against you."

"Oh, like the one that I have against you from that time you hit me? Did you tell her what you did to me?"

"I'm hanging up. Don't contact either of us again."

She had tried to warn me. I hated her for it and I wasn't quite sure why. Maybe it was because she bursted the facade of who I imagined Erik was and shattered the dream that I had found love again. Thinking back now, I probably resented her because, despite all of my attempts to ignore her words and believe Erik, I had a sinking feeling in my stomach that she was right.

I sat mesmerized by the flames engulfing the wood, growing with intensity. Our camping trip hadn't transpired as expected. This was one of the first moments of stillness since our arrival. I was taking in the silence and the warmth emanating from the fire.

After the Beth call, Erik suggested that it would be good for us to get away and reconnect. He boasted that he had a lot of camping experience. He packed the truck with all of the necessary items. We arrived right at the campsite a little before sunset. The attendant gave us our campsite, and we soon discovered that we were the only people camping. It was mid September, and the crowds had packed up for the season after Labor Day.

It was difficult to set up the campsite without light. Erik struggled to put the tent together with just the light from his cell phone. It took longer than expected. When the tent was up he began to pump air into the mattress, soon realizing that there were holes in multiple places. He insisted on doing everything himself. I sat, slowly losing patience, watching the mattress leak air.

"I haven't used this mattress in a while," he explained.

Hours later, he had attempted to locate and patch the holes with duct tape and gorilla glue, but nothing seemed to work. The night was becoming more and more frustrating. It was dark and cold and the area was desolate. This was not my idea of a fun camping trip. Every time he inflated the mattress, it would lose air within minutes. I accepted the fact that we wouldn't have an air mattress that evening, but Erik approached it with a vengeance that he was determined to settle.

"I'm hungry," I said.

"I'll get started on dinner in a few minutes." He continued fiddling with the mattress, incapable of accepting defeat.

"Why don't we just try to enjoy the night, and tomorrow we can go to the store and get another mattress?"

"Listen, I'm sorry this camping trip isn't ideal. Let me make it up to you."

"What did you have in mind?" I asked.

"Well, my friend Matt has a boat. Why don't we have a nice afternoon on the water? You can bring your friend from high school. What was her name again?"

"Claire."

"Ahhh, yes! Does that sound good?"

"It sounds perfect."

Erik brought a table and set it up with an assortment of glasses as if he were hosting a dinner party for a number of guests, yet there was just the two of us. He made a pitcher of margaritas. Our first course consisted of bruschetta. The second, steak with gorgonzola. I had never seen someone cook a gourmet meal on a camping trip. I would have settled for a cheeseburger, but Erik had to be extra, touting his chef skills and documenting the evening with pictures that he would post on social media, bragging about how great of a time we were having, even though we weren't. Everything was always showcased for appearances to provide an illusion of reality. We ate our meal and slept that night on a deflated mattress and pile of blankets.

A few hours later, I was roused by two noises that jolted me out of a deep sleep. One was Erik mumbling Beth's name, saying that he didn't mean to hurt her, and the other was the howling of coyotes nearby. I wasn't sure which was more frightening, the potential threat from the pack of wild beasts or the one lying next to me.

CHAPTER 9

I woke up sore and disoriented, reaching for my phone out of habit and quickly realizing that I didn't have one. It was somewhere at the bottom of Long Island Sound, along with Claire's keys, our phones, my bag, my license, my debit card and my dignity. It was Sunday morning. I got up to check the microwave for the time. "8:00" flashed on the display. Most people were sleeping in today or making brunch plans. In between bouts of crying, I was going on the computer to find out what time the cell phone store opened so we could replace ours. We had two hours. I felt lost without my phone and wondered how any of us ever survived without them.

A sharp pain rang through my right ear. It felt foggy and stuffed up. In the mirror, I could see a bruise appearing along my jawline where Erik struck me. My hand shook as I touched my fingertips to my face, checking the tenderness of the area. It was still difficult to accept that *it* had actually happened.

With only a few days before the transition to fall, Erik had suggested a ride on his friend Matt's boat as a last hurrah of the season.

It began as a fun Saturday on the water. Matt steadily made it out of the harbor. Music streamed through the speakers. The sun beat down on us. Our drinks spilled a little as we picked up speed, swaying from side to side with each crash of the waves. Claire grabbed her hat and held it tightly. Our bags slid across the floor of the boat. The wind blew back my hair, and I could feel the mist of the ocean against my face.

It began as an argument. He didn't like that I was talking to his friend. I wasn't paying enough attention to him. Why did I say that? What was wrong with me? He targeted my weakness, belittling me about the cellulite that I had disclosed was a source of insecurity.

"Have you seen the cottage cheese on the back of her legs?" He grabbed my hand to force me up, snatching my shorts down trying to expose my thighs.

"Erik, stop." I pushed his hand away.

His mouth continued the same verbal assault that I had suffered in private, now with an audience.

"I can't believe it's fall already. The summer always goes by so fast." I tried to ignore Erik's words and change the subject. If I didn't acknowledge it, he'd stop. I should have known better. He only escalated. The words continued, each one set on course of destruction. I searched for the man that I had fallen in love with, but those eyes that had once shown me kindness were filled with nothing but cruelty.

I stood up and guided his face towards mine to get him to snap out of this manic trance and cease fire. Once our eyes met, I said, "Erik, stop." One final plea.

His arm raised and his hand came down hard and fast against my cheek with a force that knocked me to the ground. I laid on the floor of the boat, paralyzed from the impact. And then everything went black.

When I came to, all I heard was screaming. Louder and louder, but everyone sounded so far away. Claire threw her body on top of mine to protect me from the blows, but Erik wasn't satisfied with the first hit. He kept trying to find a space in between Claire's hands and body that were shielding me to hit me again and again.

"Stop hitting her," Claire screamed while I hysterically cried. I couldn't move. I didn't want to say anything out of fear that he would hit me again.

Claire had her arms around my body. We were crouched on the floor, huddled together.

"Just ignore him. Don't respond." she whispered in my ear.

Matt finally spoke, "I'm heading in. Dude, I didn't sign up for you to hit these girls." Other than that, Matt didn't say or do anything to interfere.

The boat trip back to the marina was only a matter of minutes, but it felt like an eternity. Claire and I sat silently afraid to speak or move in fear of rousing the beast. I tried to get to an emotional place where he couldn't hurt me, almost like I was having an out-of-body experience, but his voice resonated, echoing in the distance. Crashing relentlessly like the waves. The voice that sounded so sweet before was so bitter and unrecognizable, filled with poisonous venom. Just before we entered the marina, something in Erik came alive. Intermission was over. We had entered the final act of the play.

"I'm gonna have you arrested," he exclaimed.

Claire motioned for me to stay quiet.

"I'm gonna tell the cops that you hit me," he continued.

There were no limits to the depth of cruelty this monster was willing to explore. He was emotionally bankrupt.

We got to the dock, and as soon as Erik and Matt roped up the boat, I ran. I ran and Claire followed. Erik trailed behind us screaming so loud that everyone in the apartment complex could hear him. We got to my car, and I unlocked the door. Erik was only a few steps behind us. Claire jumped in the passenger seat and locked the door. Erik tried to grab my door, but got a hold of my bag and snatched that instead. I slammed the door on him. Locked safely inside. He pounded on the windows, trying to break the glass, and kicked the sides of the car. I could see his mouth moving and spit spewing from the angry screaming, but couldn't make out what he was saying. I didn't have to. My focus was on getting us far away from him. I put the car in drive and hit the gas. Erik grabbed onto the door, but lost his grip a few feet through the parking lot. I sped away until Erik was only a blur in the rearview mirror. My eyes trained on the road heading towards safety.

⸺⧟⧟⸺

A muffled sound came from the bedroom. I peeked my head out of the bathroom to see Claire sitting up in bed. Her lips moved, but I couldn't hear what she was saying. I panicked. I shook my head vigorously back and forth as if something was lodged in my ear. I tilted my head over to the right and cupped the palm of my hand to my ear, making a suction. Nothing came out. I couldn't hear.

"I'm going to have permanent hearing loss." I yelled louder than intended since I couldn't gauge the volume.

"Shhh," Claire said, moving her pointer finger up towards her lips. She was renting a room in the guest house in an upscale suburban neighborhood. One that wasn't accustomed to police cars pulling in the driveway at 2 A.M. to inform the victim that her ex-boyfriend had bonded out. Claire had messaged the landlord back when she asked if everything was okay, saying that her girlfriend had a domestic violence incident. I was embarrassed to admit that the girlfriend was me. Tears streamed down my face. What was I going to do?

She took a black marker and wrote on a piece of paper, holding it for me to read.

Maybe you should go to the hospital and get checked out.

"I don't have my health insurance card. It was inside my phone case."

She wrote underneath the previous message.

They'll find you in the computer.

"I don't know how to get there," I said helplessly. I had always relied on the GPS app on my phone.

A few seconds later, a third message was written.

Go right out of the driveway. Right at the stop sign. Down about a mile and you'll see the hospital on the right before the high-way entrance.

"Right. Right. Right." Nothing about this situation was right. In fact, everything about it was wrong. Wrong. Wrong. I left her apartment repeating the directions in my head. *Right. Right. Right.* Ten minutes later I arrived at the Emergency Room. There was no one in the waiting room. A woman slid the window to the side.

"Can I help you?"

I paused, not knowing what to say. "My ex-boyfriend hit me yesterday and now I can't hear." Saying it out loud made it real. I started hysterically crying.

"Can I have your license and insurance card?"

"They're at the bottom of Long Island Sound."

The nurse brought me into a room and began asking me questions for the assessment.

"Is this the first time he's hit you?"

I nodded in the affirmative. Tears streamed down my face. I brushed them away, embarrassed by my appearance. My fingers got tangled in the hair framing my face, still windblown and salty. I hadn't showered. I hadn't slept. I shook, rocking back and forth to try and control it, soon realizing everything was out of my control. The motion brought me back to a memory of the waves consuming my belongings. Lying on the floor of the boat, I saw my bag thrown overboard, then my phone, and finally the card with my dog's paw print on it that was tucked inside my wallet. The only thing that I had left of her was floating along on the surface. Drifting farther and farther away from the boat. Out of reach.

"Do you live together?"

"No."

"Does he have access to your home?"

"Yes."

"I strongly suggest you have the locks changed."

I burst into tears holding my face in my hands, leaning over my knees. "Why is this happening?" I wailed, desperately thinking back to the way Erik had attacked me on the boat.

The nurse bent down to meet my eyes. She held my knees, balancing herself, waiting for me to make eye contact, and said, "I know you love him and you're in shock right now, but I want you to promise me something."

I nodded.

"You have to promise that you won't take him back."

"He doesn't want me anyway," I said, crying harder at the prospect that I was tossed away like an old sweater.

"Oh, believe me, that would be the best-case scenario, if he just went away and left you alone, but more than likely, he won't. He'll come back and give you a sob story, telling you he's sorry and that he'll never do it again. He will."

"How do you know this?" I asked.

"Because I've lived it," she said. "My ex-husband was a mean son-of-a-bitch. His rage was intensified by his drinking. I suffered for ten years because I didn't think I was strong enough to leave. I didn't think I deserved anything better. You're young. You're a beautiful girl. Don't make the same mistakes that I did."

"I just can't believe this happened. Did I do something wrong? Maybe if I hadn't talked to his friend. Or maybe if I hadn't made that comment. I wouldn't be here now."

"Sweetheart, this is not your fault. Don't you dare take the blame for this man's actions. He made the choice to hit you, and I promise you that if you stay, he'll do it again. You might not be so lucky next time."

She took my hand in hers and squeezed it tightly. "You're going to be okay. You'll get through this."

I looked at the ground feeling lost and alone, but most of all, ashamed. *Who had I become?*

After a few more questions, the intake nurse escorted me to the examination room. She asked me to lie down on the table.

"Another nurse will be in shortly. Remember what I said. Hang in there."

She left, closing the door behind her. A few moments later, a knock on the door.

"Hi, Dana. I'm Shannon. Can you tell me what happened?"

I repeated the story again and cried just as much as I did the first time, reliving the experience with each word.

"I'm sorry that happened to you," she said comfortingly. "If you don't mind, I'm going to feel around and see if you have any major injuries. Is that okay?"

"Yes," I said.

She began moving around my abdomen, pushing in, checking for tenderness. She slowly made her way up and down my body towards my head.

"What symptoms are you experiencing?" She asked.

"A broken heart," I said inconsolably.

She looked at me with sadness in her eyes. "I know this is so hard right now." She put her hand on my shoulder to reassure me. "I noticed a few scrapes and bruises. Good news, it doesn't seem like you have any internal injuries."

She touched my jaw line and I winced in pain.

"It doesn't look like anything is broken. Just tender from the impact. We won't know for sure unless we take X-rays."

"I don't want any X-rays," I said.

"You don't have to do anything you don't want to," she assured me. "I'm going to check inside your ear now, since I was told you complained about it when you checked in."

She put the instrument in my right ear and my left. "I don't see anything abnormal. How does it feel?"

"It feels blocked, like I'm in a tunnel."

"Let's hope that goes away in a few days."

"Let's hope," I repeated robotically.

I started to cry. The nurse gently rubbed my back. "I was in an abusive relationship once. I know what you're going through.

It doesn't get better either. You want to believe that he'll change, but it only gets worse. If you stay with him, this won't be the last time he hurts you. Please remember that you're not alone. One in three women have experienced some form of physical violence by an intimate partner."

In the span of thirty minutes, I had met two professional women who had confided in me that they had been in abusive relationships. It made me think about how violence is so prevalent in our culture that these types of incidents have been experienced by so many. Almost normalized. I felt sick to be part of the statistic.

"I'd like to go home now, if that's okay," I said timidly, sounding more like a little girl than a grown woman.

"Of course. Just give me a few minutes to get the paperwork together, and you'll be on your way."

A few minutes later, another woman came into the room to deliver my discharge paperwork. I waited, expecting her to share her story of violence too, but all she did was hand me the papers and a card with information. "Please call this number if you'd like to talk with someone. There are many services out there to help victims."

I took the paperwork and choked out a thank you. Swallowing hard. I was now categorized as a victim. I thought back to Diedre's story from my writing group. How I was sure that I'd never be like her. Look at me now. We weren't so different after all.

CHAPTER 10

The car ride home was unbearable. I messaged Mia telling her what happened on the boat.

I'm so sorry, Dana

This is a nightmare!

I love you. I'm here.
You're strong.
Remember you deserve better.

Thanks with a kiss emoji

Call me when you feel like talking

I'm emotionally exhausted

I get it. Rest up. We'll talk soon.

Love you

Love you more

———⊶∞⊷———

The next few days were torture. His cologne still lingered on my pillow like the feelings that I still held and the memory of the future plans he had made for us. I isolated, ashamed of what had happened to me. I'd look at my phone screen every few seconds, hoping to see an envelope indicating a text message from him, but there was nothing but radio silence. I felt depleted. I cried an ocean of tears waiting for him to return. The phone finally buzzed. A glimmer of hope faded when I saw it was just Mia sending another motivational quote. All of the motivational quotes in the world wouldn't pull me out of this funk.

Why didn't he love me?

Old trauma wounds of abandonment had been reopened. My heart pounded thinking back to how angry he was and how frightened I was. I wanted desperately to go back to the beginning, but I knew that was nearly impossible. He sold me a version of him that wasn't true. I fell in love with an idea that didn't exist. I sat in that space filled with anguish and heartache, hoping that the one who had inflicted the pain could alleviate it.

Aimee is my therapist, but she feels more like a friend. She's the only therapist that I've ever met who I actually believe gives a damn, and I've met a lot of therapists.

The last one I saw for a short period of time was a total whack job, which made me wonder if he was the one that needed therapy. It was right after I started having panic attacks. At first I thought I was having a heart attack. After the cardiologist determined I had a healthy heart, he recommended I see a pulmonologist. My lungs were fine, so the doctor suggested a gastroenterologist, who found nothing wrong with me. When everyone had had a turn experimenting on me, the doctors concluded that there was nothing physically wrong, so I was referred to a psychiatrist.

Enter Dr. Douche, who claimed to specialize in panic disorders. Dr. Douche believed in self-fulling prophecy and mastication. No, I didn't misunderstand him. He meant mastication, not masturbation. If he advocated for masturbation I might have agreed with him, but that wasn't the case. I was feeling uneasy about a vacation I was going on because I didn't want to have an attack while away.

I expressed my concern. "I'm so scared that I'll have a panic attack on the trip and ruin our vacation."

Dr. Douche looked blankly at me and said, without any ounce of empathy, "If you think you'll ruin your trip then you'll ruin your trip."

He also believed that mastication was the cure for anxiety, and instead of walking away with a Xanax prescription, he told me to, "go to the grocery store, buy a steak, cook it well done, chew every piece of meat, and notice how masticating alleviates anxiety." If you ask me, he was the crazy one, because what normal person would cook a steak well done? I didn't see Dr. Douche after that.

Finding a therapist is like cultivating a relationship. It has to be a good fit or it doesn't work. I didn't find it with Dr. Douche.

But Aimee was different. She never said, "times up" when I was in the middle of a sob story, forced to save my tears for the next time. She always told me that I could contact her in between sessions if I needed to. Considering what I'd been through, there were a few times that I took her up on the offer.

I know I should have been, but I wasn't initially honest about the boat incident with Aimee. I told her that Erik could be verbally abusive, but I didn't tell her he hit me. It wasn't that I didn't think I could trust her. I knew I could. I think it had more to do with me actually admitting to myself that it had happened. When I had talked to her about Erik's rage in the past, she never once discredited my feelings or encouraged me to leave. She just helped me work through how I was feeling and made me feel less alone in the world.

"Doesn't life just fucking suck sometimes?" she asked. I loved when she swore. I thought it made her more human and relatable. And she was right, because now was one of the times when life did suck. It fucking sucked.

I expected to never hear from Erik again. As the days went by, I cried a little less and felt a little stronger. The pain wasn't as excruciating. It was bearable. But then one day, everything changed.

He showed up at my house, asking if we could talk. I should have slammed the door. I should have turned my back on him and told him to leave. I should have called the police, especially since there was a protective order that was automatically put in place after the attack. It banned him from coming near me or my home.

But I didn't.

"Please, I don't expect you to forgive me, but I needed to see you. I'm sorry, Dana." He spoke softly. Tears began to stream down his face.

I listened, making sure to keep a distance from him.

"I'm not that monster. I don't know why I did that. I started researching online, and I think I have Intermittent Explosive Disorder. I also think back to all the times I've been out of control, and alcohol has always been a factor. I promise you I'm not that guy. I'm going to change. I'm going to stop drinking. I need to make this better. I'll prove it to you."

He fell to the ground on his knees, looking desperately at me, holding my legs and sobbing.

"Please forgive me. I can't live without you."

"I can't teach you how to be a good man."

"I know. I know. I promise I'll change."

With tears in his eyes and sweat caked hair, he looked at me like a broken man in anguish. The green had returned to his eyes. No longer filled with rage, his eyes looked gentle. I wondered how they could change so drastically. It's like he was two different people. I wanted to keep this version of him.

Love makes you overlook the flaws and ignore the red flags. Deep down inside I knew I shouldn't have taken him back, but I wasn't strong enough to turn him away. I loved him. I had been so love sick the past few days. I just wanted it to go away. I wanted to believe that he made a mistake and could change. That the way he acted on the boat wasn't the real him. That he could be the man I once knew. I pulled him up from his knees and hugged him tightly. Too tight, not wanting to lose anything else. I had lost my father. I had lost Peter. Two significant men in my life. I couldn't lose Erik. He kissed me tenderly on the forehead. *We could do this.* Together. We would fix this.

CHAPTER 11

After that, Erik was on his best behavior. It felt like the beginning again. He was committed to his therapy. He wasn't drinking. His mood seemed lighter. Like whatever was haunting him had exited. I felt like we could have a fresh start. It continued like that for a couple of weeks until I began asking him about fixing the bathroom. He had promised that he would fix the window, and now months later, not only was the window still not fixed, but the condition of the bathroom was getting worse. I was losing patience.

One night, the incessant banging woke me up. In his Addereal-induced state it wasn't unusual for Erik to stay up all night cleaning the kitchen, organizing the spices, masturbating to a porn marathon, but tonight his focus was the infamous bathroom renovation. Renovation implied that something was actually being created, but now, ninety days since he began, nothing had been done. I use the term bathroom loosely, because it wasn't actually a bathroom anymore. It was beams with no insulation or drywall. There was no toilet. No sink, no mirror, no cabinet, no light fixtures. Nothing. It looked more like an outhouse than a bathroom. He wasted time watching YouTube videos, thinking that he would learn how to remodel a bathroom from a few tutorials. He drew out sketches of the layout as if he were an architect. Every morning he'd say, "today is the day I'm going to finish the bathroom." And every night it looked exactly the same.

I checked my phone. It was 2 A.M. and he was banging downstairs. Who in their right mind would think it was okay to do construction at 2 A.M.? The guy had absolutely no rational sense or regard for others. "Eriiiiik," I called downstairs, but of course he couldn't hear me over the banging. I begrudgingly got up from bed to confront him. I walked downstairs, bracing myself for what I was about to see. He had earbuds in. I stepped over a pile of what looked like what once were pieces of the wall. I waved my hand to get his attention. He removed an earbud from his ear and gave me a look of irritation.

"Stop banging. I'm trying to sleep."

He took a deep breath and let out a long exhale. "I need to get this done," he said as if I were interrupting an artist creating a masterpiece on a blank canvas. Who was I to interfere with genius? But this was not the Sistine Chapel. This was an empty box that needed to be made functional. This was a violation. This was my home. I peeked inside this empty space, feeling helpless. This was beyond frustrating. It was a nightmare. It would cost me at least five thousand dollars to get someone in here to fix the mess he made. Why should I have to pay out of pocket for something that I didn't even ask for, didn't even know about? That's why I tried to be patient with him, because I felt like he was my only option.

He dragged it out on purpose, partly because he had no clue what he was doing, and partly because when he finished the bathroom, I wouldn't have any use for him. I was at his mercy, and that's exactly where he wanted me. As always, Erik had a way to flip the narrative to make it seem like he was helping when he was really harming.

"You know, I'm doing you a favor, because I found a nest in the wall and you could have an infestation. You don't want that, do you? Also, I need to make sure that everything is up to code in case one day you want to sell the house. You wouldn't want to run into a problem, would you?"

He chewed on his fingers in between speaking. He smelled like menthol cigarettes and regret.

"This is crazy, Erik. All I asked you to do was replace the window, not the entire bathroom. I didn't give you permission to destroy my bathroom. I didn't need a remodel. You took it upon yourself and lied to me about it. You locked me out of my space. You did most of the destruction while I was sleeping and got rid of the evidence so I wouldn't question you. All this time the door was locked, I thought you were replacing the window and maybe decorating the bathroom with beach décor like we had discussed. This is insane! You said you wanted to surprise me. This is one big fucking unauthorized surprise. What a mess! You're driving me crazy with the banging and the promises that you're going to fix it. You're incapable of fixing anything. The only thing you're capable of is destroying things."

"Maybe I want to drive you crazy. Did you ever think of that? Maybe that's the goal."

And that was it. I saw it. The mask had slipped. He had revealed himself. He couldn't maintain the façade.

"I can't fucking look at you or deal with you. You don't make any sense." He stood there with a hammer in his hand and a lit cigarette hanging from his mouth. He was caked with dirt from his face to under his fingertips. His clothes were stained with white powder from the sheetrock.

I stared into his weary, soulless eyes. I couldn't bear to expend another minute of energy investing in this conversation that was going nowhere. His words fell silent, floating to the kitchen floor like rain drops on the pavement. Disappearing in the cracks of the tiles, I waited for them to cease into a meaningless abyss, like the empty promises that he made. Time ticked in tortured beats that could never be recovered. Sometimes he wrapped his words in pretty packages with red bows of longing and hope. But times like these, I heard the ones that were thrown like daggers in the heat of anger, echoing through the walls of my psyche. The ones that cut my heart into pieces, pushing down hard on the blade so that I felt each slice with the same intensity as the first. The ones intended to destroy me were the ones that numbed me from more pain. As I became more accustomed to the attacks, my armor grew stronger, protecting me from the shrapnel of insults.

Without another word, I stormed upstairs and got back in bed. I put a pillow over my head to drown out the banging. Something had to give, but nothing was going to be accomplished at this hour.

Almost as if Mia could sense it, she messaged me.

Any updates with your window?

Nothing yet. I'm so frustrated!

Dana, that's your house! Why don't you hire someone if he can't do it?

*He swears he can do it and
asked me to give him a chance
to show me.*

Gurl, I wouldn't wait too long. That's not safe.

*I know. I know. He keeps
assuring me that he'll get it
done. Fingers crossed.*

Well, I hope he's not all talk.

Me too!

Okay, let's catch up later

Okie dokie.

I couldn't bring myself to disclose to Mia what just happened, so I glazed over it. Partly because I was embarrassed, and partly because I was still trying to wrap my head around it.

CHAPTER 12

Erik knew that I had a telehealth call with Aimee. I wasn't feeling well and not up for going to the office. He agreed to go for a drive so I'd have some privacy.

"How's everything, Dana?" Aimee's steady voice calmed me.

"Hold on a second," I said. I checked the blinds to see if Erik had left and I was free to speak. His Jeep wasn't parked in front of the house.

"Everything alright?" Aimee asked.

"Sorry, I was just making sure Erik left."

"Tell me about how you're feeling."

"I'm on edge," I said. I could feel myself shaking. It was difficult to relax.

"What's going on?"

"Erik has been keeping me up at night. I can't sleep. He's constantly accusing me of cheating on him and doing other things to sabotage my peace."

"Why do you stay?"

"I want to help him. I feel bad. I know he doesn't mean it when he lashes out at me. I keep trying to rationalize why he does what he does or says what he says. I started researching the cycle of abuse and narcissistic personality traits. I find myself going down the rabbit hole in the advice forums. It's crazy how many people have experienced a situation similar to mine."

"I think we need to start focusing on you and less on Erik. Think about ways that we can build you up and get your needs met. Erik is not your whole world. He's just a piece of your world. Let's brainstorm ways that we can value you."

The teacher in me wanted to understand him. I had built a career on reaching at-risk kids. But Erik wasn't a kid. This was different. I thought that if I gave him more, he would get better. Yet the more I gave him, the more he resented me for it. I realized that you can't expect to get anything from an empty vessel. I thought if I fixed him, I might heal my own wounds left from a lifetime of disappointment and father hunger. I was wrong. It wasn't my job to mother him. I wasn't his psychologist or life coach. I was his girlfriend, and that is all I ever needed to be. As the situation grew uglier, I adopted more roles. When his behavior got worse, I tried harder, did better, gave more, but it never worked. It was unmanageable, and eventually it became too much to bear. I knew that if something didn't happen, I would lose myself. This time for good. I wanted to believe him every time he promised me it would get better, but I knew deep down inside that it wouldn't. I stayed too long waiting for him to change back to the man I fell in love with as if I were waiting for the next train to arrive, but soon realizing that I was at the wrong track.

<hr />

Erik had insisted on treating me to a vacation for my birthday. A feeling of impending doom led up to the trip. The forecast called for rain in South Florida. He had gotten a message from the landlord saying that he had to vacate his apartment for what I found out later was due to his inability to pay his rent. He was six months behind. This was not how I intended to celebrate my fortieth birthday. He had arranged a car service to drive us to the airport. A friend that he used to work for would do it. His name was Walter. He was a seventy-something-year-old gay black man who had a very unusual relationship with Erik. From my understanding, Walter was wealthy and had done well by establishing himself as a premiere car service in the Fairfield County area. Erik had met him at a local coffee shop, and the two hit it off. Erik, I'm sure, had smelled money on him and targeted him by turning on the charm and sizing him up for what he could get. I realized later that Erik was a parasite, always looking for a new host. I didn't understand why Erik and Walter had a falling out, but it was clear Erik was trying to rekindle their relationship. I overheard him on the phone making arrangements for the trip.

"Yes, Daddy. We would love it if you could bring us to the airport on Thursday afternoon and pick us up on Tuesday morning."

I listened, wondering why he just called him 'Daddy.'

"$150? No problem," Erik continued. "I'm still your Baby Boy."

This was weird. I had to say something.

"Erik, what's up with you calling him 'Daddy?'"

"Oh, that's just something we do."

"Really, because it's kind of strange to me that you'd call a seventy-year-old gay man 'Daddy' and he calls you 'Baby Boy?'"

"It's really nothing, Dana. There you go again, being judgemental. I'm sure you have nicknames that you call your friends."

"You're right. I do, but 'Daddy' isn't one of them."

Walter arrived at the designated time, ready to bring us to the airport. He was a skinny, frail-looking man. Erik had mentioned that he had been battling cancer, which would account for his appearance. He was quiet and stoic. I thanked him for coming, and he didn't even look at me or reply. He just took the keys and got in the car. I thought maybe he was having a bad day and didn't think much more about it. Erik and I sat together in the back seat of my car as Walter drove us toward LaGuardia airport. Erik monopolized the conversation, gushing over me, bragging to Walter about how happy he was with his beautiful author girlfriend. Walter held tightly to the steering wheel, his eyes focused on the highway and listened silently.

"We've had such an amazing time together. My only regret is that I hadn't met her sooner," he said. "Mark my words, she's my end game. I've found my soulmate."

Everything he said was so over-the-top. It didn't sound authentic. I wanted him to stop, but I just tuned him out and stared out the window, watching the cars blur as we passed by, every minute growing more anxious that something wasn't right. When we got off the exit, I tuned out Erik's voice and got lost in the sounds of the city. Erik held my hand, and Walter finally met my eyes in the rearview mirror. Erik asked him about business. Walter answered with one-word responses.

"I really think that I can add to your revenue. I have some fantastic ideas I'd love to run by you. Let's sit down for lunch and see how I can use my finance background and extensive research skills to expand your business," he pitched the old man. The car ride was less than an hour long, but it felt longer with Erik's long-winded monologue. I think we all would have preferred to sit in silence or just listen to the radio. When we arrived, I took my luggage and went to the curb. Erik stood behind. He said he had to talk to Walter. I watched as Erik whispered something to Walter in his ear. Walter's expression showed he was visibly upset. His forehead wrinkled, and he shook his head. Erik put his hand on Walter's shoulder reassuringly, but Walter shrugged him off, got in the car quickly, and pulled away without a nod or a wave.

"What's wrong with him?" I asked.

"Who knows. Faggots are always so emotional." He pulled his luggage onto the curb and motioned for me to follow him into the airport, not looking back.

CHAPTER 13

We lined up by Zone, Erik staring me down with a look of disgust, a twisted smirk on his face. He casually popped pieces of chocolate in his mouth without a care in the world and scanned the line. A young blond girl got behind him. Her breasts spilled out of her camisole. She was 20-something. And traveling alone. Erik took notice. He liked them young. They were easy targets.

"Are you visiting friends in Fort Lauderdale?" he asked her. She smiled and nodded.

"Have you been there before?"

"Yes. I go a lot. How about you?"

"Me too. I travel there for business."

He was sticking to the lie, and in character. He smiled wide and was enthusiastic. So friendly. So complimentary. I could understand why the girl would fall for his charm. I was once that girl. Erik was trying to get a rise out of me, blatantly flirting with her in front of me. I was familiar with his game. He had done it so many times before. The waitress at the restaurant. The clerk at the store. The guest at the hotel. Erik was the ever-so-charming, irresistible, dashing man. His goal was to make me feel small by disrespecting me under the guise that he was just being friendly. It was always women. It was always young, beautiful women. If I protested, I was jealous and insecure. I knew not to react, because that was what he was looking for. So I stood as a silent prisoner, trapped inside my body, training myself to be disciplined. We made our way onto the plane, and Erik continued to talk to the girl, ignoring the fact that we were together. He even assisted her with placing her carry-on bag in the overhead, making sure to move his face within inches of her breasts as he looked back at me with a smirk.

"Thank you for your help."

"Have a great flight," he said to her before settling down in the seat next to me.

"How are you, daaaling?" he asked, searching my face for any signs of distress.

I wouldn't give him the satisfaction. "I'm fine."

He leaned over so no one could hear, and said, "You might not come home from this trip. Stranger things have happened."

I shuttered. "That's not funny."

He smirked with his sideways smile, "It's not supposed to be." He popped a pretzel into his mouth, put his ear buds in, and selected a movie.

Something about getting off the plane in paradise made traveling with a psychopath a little easier to manage. Sunshine. Palm trees. A warm ocean breeze. The vibrant colors of South Florida. I felt renewed.

"I'm going to give you the best birthday ever," Erik said.

Considering his track record, I had a feeling that wasn't the case, but I went with it. A short Uber ride to the Airbnb, and the weather had changed. The sky was dark and ominous. Foreboding storm clouds loomed in the distance. The wind whipped wildly. The rain poured down in menacing torrents. We had arrived just in time for a tropical storm. I would be stuck in the rental with Erik for the next five days. Erik was ordering my presents online to be delivered at our temporary address and was preoccupied with making sure they would arrive in time. We were staying in a duplex, and since Erik was prone to regular outburst, I was afraid that the couple next door would hear us. And as expected, on the first night when something didn't go his way, Erik started yelling like a toddler having a tantrum. No one said anything.

By day two, I was over him and his antics. That night, we went to one of my favorite Peruvian restaurants. The conversation started off well. The food was delicious. I relaxed, thinking that for once we might actually have a good time.

I was wrong.

Erik appeared laid back at first, but there was something always brewing under the surface, ready to erupt at the slightest provocation. I was constantly walking on eggshells. We were talking about relationships. I had just started a dating column and was sharing one of the stories that someone submitted. I was trying to maintain my professionalism as a dating expert, but failing miserably in my personal life. I felt like a fraud, but I shared the story with Erik.

"What makes you a dating expert?" He asked. "How sad are these people that have to ask you for advice?"

"Ouch," I said. "I'm honored that people trust me to help them with their relationship issues."

"Are you even qualified to do so? Oh, that's right, you've slept with everyone in South Florida. That must make you an expert." He sneered with a sinister look.

I was not going to sit at dinner and take this abuse, so without another word, I got up, walked out, and ordered an uber. He paid the check and followed me out of the restaurant, complaining about how embarrassing it was for me to leave him sitting alone at the table. There wasn't an off switch with Erik. When he got going, he never stopped until I was in tears. The same cycle continued.

The next morning, my birthday, I awoke to him smiling at me, warmly.

"Happy birthday, princess," he said. Balloons were hung up with a banner. He got me a crown.

"Your presents are coming throughout the day, but here are some cards to get you started." He handed me four cards and kissed me on the forehead.

"I got you a card for every decade," he said.

Inside each card, he wrote about how smart and talented I was. He complimented me on my strength and beauty. He said I was funny and fun and creative. All the things that he had said in the beginning of our relationship. Everything that he had admired in me that was now turned around to weaponize. As I read each card over and over, I thought about how sweet he was, and how loved and appreciated I felt. The feeling was fleeting, and I knew that Erik would find some way to ruin it. He always did. He made me a beautiful steak dinner and a special chocolate cake. I was drinking more and more to deal with him, never knowing the next time he would explode and the consequences I would have to pay. The price for love cost more each time.

The rain inundated us with a ferocity that prevented us from doing anything outside. He wasn't drinking, or so I thought, because after the boat incident, he swore he wouldn't. The Airbnb host left a bottle of wine. He had a couple of glasses, and I saw his mood change instantly.

He said he had to go to the store, and when he was gone for over an hour, I went out to find him. He wasn't picking up his phone. I had a feeling he was at this hole-in-the wall bar near the rental. It was the only place within walking distance.

The door was open. It was dark and smoky inside. There were a few old people that looked like they had been sitting in the same place for the past thirty years collecting dust. Just as I had suspected, Erik was standing against the bar with a rocks glass full of a whiskey-like, brown substance. He saw me and looked shocked, grabbed the whiskey and swallowed it in one gulp.

"You're kidding me, right," I said to him.

For once, he had nothing to say.

I turned to the bartender. "He's going to need the tab."

The old men at the bar laughed and told me to relax. I said he wasn't supposed to drink with his medication. Erik was still silent. I could tell the alcohol was taking an effect on him. While he was paying the tab, I swiped his phone without him seeing. He stumbled out of the bar after me, finally coming to life, yelling inarticulately about me embarrassing him. As if he had to keep appearances with the local degenerates.

It was seldom that I had his unlocked phone, and I wanted to take advantage of the short time that I had it. He was splashing behind me in the rain, yelling. I saw a text from Walter saying that he wouldn't be able to pick us up at the airport because Erik hadn't paid him and that he was going to leave my key on the tire of my vehicle. We had to find an alternative way to get home. I took a picture of the message so that I would have Walter's number. Then, I looked at Erik's contacts. There were hundreds, mostly women with just a first name, followed by a dating app where he connected with them: Amy Tinder, Ann Tinder, Ashley Match, Auden Bumble. I also saw a South Florida area code and called the number, not knowing who it could be. Moments later, the voice of an older woman answered.

"How do you know Erik?" I asked, not wanting to waste time with formalities.

"He dated my daughter."

"Who is your daughter?"

"Beth."

Beth was the woman who had tried to warn me.

"Are you with him now?" she asked.

"Yes."

"Are you okay?"

"No."

"Can you just leave and get away from him?"

That was the million dollar question. Her words ruminated in my head long after the call ended. *Could I just leave? Would he let me go if I tried?* The answer remained to be seen. One thing I knew for certain, was that I was paying the price for not heeding Beth's warning. I realized now, she was only trying to spare me from the same abuse that she had suffered. Some lessons were learned the hard way.

CHAPTER 14

"Where is my phone?" Erik yelled. "I think I left it at the bar."

"I have it. I grabbed it for you so you wouldn't leave it behind." I said, making sure to delete the recent phone call before handing it over to him.

"You're up to something, you fucking bitch."

"Fuck you, Erik."

I got away from Erik long enough to call Walter, asking what the issue was with picking us up from the airport.

"We had an agreement. He was supposed to pay me when I dropped you off." Walter's voice shook with anger. "When we got there, he told me he'd give me the money when he came back."

That must have been what he was whispering in his ear which explains the angry expression from Walter.

"Why is it that big of a deal if he pays you before or after the service?" I didn't understand the tension between them.

"It's the principle that we had an agreement, and he knew the terms. See…you don't know Erik. He thinks he can get away with pushing the boundaries. I knew that I shouldn't have taken this job. It's not worth the headache. He's crossed me too many times, and honestly, I'm not taking anymore of his abuse."

"Abuse? What exactly do you mean?" I probed.

"I shouldn't be telling you this, but…Erik has had, um, let's say a few outbursts. He's shown up at my house late at night, screaming obscenities. He's destroyed my property. One time I didn't answer the door, and I looked out the window to see him pulling my plants out of the garden and knocking down my outdoor furniture. All in the rain, mud covered, a displaced look in his eyes."

I knew exactly what he was talking about. I had seen that look before.

Walter continued. "I'd given him too many chances and finally had to let him go when he was inappropriate with my clients' granddaughter."

"Inappropriate? How?" I asked, bracing myself for answers I didn't want to hear.

"It was discovered that he was soliciting sex from her while driving her to the airport."

I was careful not to interrupt. I wanted to hear everything he had to say.

"He told her that he'd get her a fake ID and take her to the bar. He was caught sexting her. The girl was only sixteen-years-old."

"Oh my God." I gasped.

"He has a major issue. I felt sorry for him. You know him enough to see that he has a way of making people feel sympathetic towards him. When he's good, he's very charming and everyone wants to be around him, but when he's bad, watch out. I've given him too many chances, but he takes advantage. I can't be associated with him."

"I'm so sorry that happened to you. I completely understand. Thank you for explaining it to me."

"If you were smart, you'd get away from him."

"Can I pay you for the ride there?"

"No, I don't want your money. Please don't contact me ever again." He hung up abruptly.

⸺⸻⸺

I couldn't wait for Erik to get out of the shower. I had to confront him with this new information.

"I just got off the phone with Walter. He said he's not picking us up from the airport."

"Not picking us up?" he peeked his head out of the shower pushing the shower curtain aside. "That man is such a pain in the ass."

"Yeah, I guess Daddy isn't too happy with Baby Boy."

"Alexa, lower the music." Alexa obediently decreased the sound of the song. It was the one talking about fucking someone like an animal, which I thought was particularly relevant, considering Erik's recently discovered perversions.

"That's really the least of your problems. He claims that he fired you from working for him because you were solicitating sex from an underaged girl."

"Liarrrr." He yelled. I heard him twist the water off, and he stepped out of the shower still covered in suds. "Both of you will learn not to cross me. You mess with the bull, you get the horns."

"She was only 16, Erik."

"She was in college. Didn't you ever hook up with someone that was older than you when you were in college?"

"You're old enough to be her father, Erik."

"Don't judge me. Everyone likes younger women. Men have been with younger women since the beginning of time."

"Women, Erik. Not children. There's a difference. Everyone doesn't like having sex with children."

"I'm calling the motherfucker. Who does he think he is, spreading lies? I bet you believe him too, right? Of course you believe him. You're never on my side."

"He has no reason to lie. First Beth and now Walter. You act like there's a big conspiracy against you. Even if she was in college, which I'm pretty sure she wasn't. Your job was to drive her to the airport. Not to get in her pants."

I followed him out of the bathroom. Water dripped off his naked body along with patches of soap suds in blotches that he hadn't washed off. He grabbed his phone and started texting furiously. In between angry texts, he toweled off, shaking his head and muttering under his breath and quickly threw on a t-shirt and shorts.

"I don't need this shit. I'm going out."

"Wonderful." I said.

"I'm going to fuck everyone."

"Is that right? Do you mean everyone or just the 16-year-old girls?"

He responded by throwing a chair across the room. Lucky hid under the table, shaking in the corner.

Erik didn't make it far on his quest to fuck everyone. I couldn't have been that lucky. He made it outside and turned around. Thinking better of it because of the weather or perhaps he just wanted to torture me more.

The rain came down, flooding the streets. Soaked from head to toe, he jumped maniacally through the puddles, a grocery bag in one hand, a lit cigarette in the other. His hair slicked back; a white t-shirt plastered to his body.

"You think you're gonna find someone to replace me," he screamed. "I'll find someone on Tinder to sleep with. In fact, I'll hook up with everyone within a 5-mile radius." His go-to threat was saying he'd leave me to hook up with someone on Tinder. "You're used up and old. No one wants you anyway."

He waited for my reaction with a crooked grin on his face intent on hurting me. It was my birthday weekend. I was turning forty years old, and he wanted to remind me that I was reaching my expiration date and could easily be traded in for a younger model like an old car that had too many miles on it. He had a way of making me feel like I should be grateful to at least have someone, even if that someone was an abusive psychopath.

"I wish you would," I said and meant it. He was like a cancer that spread its insidious wrath wherever it went. I knew that if I continued down this path, he would be my demise. I had to save myself. I ran back into the apartment, his screams muffled by the rain. His flip flops grew louder on the pavement as he chased closely behind me. I quickly shut the door, making sure it was locked, and bolted. He slammed his hand against the door. I was relieved it was an object and not my face. This time.

"Let me in, Dana. You can't keep me out here."

"Go away, Erik."

He pounded on the door.

"I said let me in. You stupid bitch."

The pounding grew louder. Rapid and steadily increasing like my heartbeat.

I looked to the corner of the living area. Lucky sat shaking under the table. I had never seen him shake before.

I didn't want him to alarm the neighbors, so I cracked the door to prevent him from causing a scene. He shoved his way in. I grabbed my phone and dialed 9-1-1.

He swatted the phone out of my hand and said to the dispatcher, "Sorry, my child was playing with my cell and accidentally dialed. I apologize for that. It won't happen again." He pulled the phone away and looked at me, pretending I was his child, and part of me felt like I was. "Darling, I told you that you can't play around with the emergency number. You know this prank call could have taken away from helping someone who really needed it."

I stood frozen with fear thinking, *But I need help. Help me.*

He continued with his ruse, "No, you don't have to send anyone. I'll talk to my daughter about being more careful. You have a good day too." He hung up and threw the phone to the ground. Anywhere else, the cops would have actually investigated the call, but this was South Florida. No one was coming.

He pushed me up against the door. Pressing my body firmly against his. I could smell alcohol and stale cigarettes on his breath. After the boat incident, he swore he'd never drink again, blaming his violence on the mix of alcohol with his medication. By this time, I should have known better than to believe anything he said. He grabbed my face hard, directing my eyes to his. "If you pull anything like that again, I promise you it won't end well." And that promise I believed.

After that, I felt like I was sleepwalking. The rain continued to fall in torrents. The Sunshine State had never had less sun. There was a gloom to it that lingered ominously. I prayed it wasn't a sign. He said he was going to take a shower, since he was all wet because of me. I had learned quickly that everything was my fault. It was in my best interest to keep quiet. He would never accept blame. His words twisted and turned like a top, eventually getting to a point where I started to believe that maybe he was right.

That night he tried to kill himself by swallowing an entire bottle of pills. He lay stiff on the couch. I thought he was dead. While part of me was relieved that I would finally be done with this monster, the other didn't want to be responsible for having a dead boyfriend in the Airbnb. I hovered over his chest, waiting for it to rise and fall. Placing my face over his, I noticed air expelling from his nostrils. I tapped his face to wake him. He moaned. Opening his eyes, he looked at me and said, "You're so beautiful. You look like an angel."

"What did you take?" I searched his prescription pill bottles. Nothing looked like it was missing. He pointed to a bottle on the counter. I grabbed it and read the label, 'Melatonin.' I laughed to myself. *He tried to overdose on Melatonin.* I quickly Googled if that was even possible. After a search, I discovered that a person couldn't die from too much Melatonin. *The asshole couldn't even kill himself right.* I wanted to leave so badly, but I felt horrible leaving him behind. My conscience wouldn't allow it. He needed help. I swore that I would get us back home and then find a facility for him.

He'd probably get the best sleep of his life. For once, maybe I would too. He murmured and adjusted his position, rolling on his side. A slight snore-like a sputtering motor came from him. I rubbed his back. He knew that I was close to leaving and played on my emotions to get me to stay. His pathetic suicide attempt by melatonin was despicable, but it got the intended outcome. I stayed.

"Everything will be okay." As soon as I said the words, I wanted to take them back. Now, he wasn't the only one who was lying to me. I was lying to myself.

CHAPTER 15

"Fear as a child becomes rage as an adult," he said

"What do you mean, Erik?"

The fallen leaves on the ground marked the change in seasons. I shivered from the brisk breeze, signaling autumn approaching. He motioned me to sit on his lap. I stroked his hair as he wrapped his arms around my waist, tightly holding on.

"What did he do to you?" I asked. It had always been implied that he had suffered some abuse from his father, but he had never come right out and said it. Some things don't need to be said to be understood.

He looked down at the ground and paused. When he brought his head back up, tears had formed in his eyes, and instead of hiding them, he looked at me vulnerably. If he could have said a word in that moment, it would have been "help." I was a teacher. I was a caretaker. All I did was help people. And I loved him.

How could I not help him?

It was Wednesday morning, and that meant that the long-awaited time for our weekly session had arrived. I waited outside of Aimee's door, flipping through magazines, alternating between stew recipes to warm the winter woes and seven red flags to know if you're dating a sociopath. Indeed, the universe had a sense of humor.

The noise machine sat on the floor, and although it did its job blocking out intelligible conversations, I could still hear faint sounds coming from behind the door. I wondered about the woman inside the room. What prompted her to seek therapy? Maybe she was complaining about having to clean her own bathroom because the housekeeper was sick. Maybe the stress that accompanies planning a dinner party for ten prominent members of the community had gotten the best of her. I could hear ruffling and the voices behind the door grew louder. The knob turned, and when the woman exited, my eyes were focused on reading the article about sociopathic behavior. Lying effortlessly was one of the indicators mentioned. Lying becomes a natural response, akin to breathing. Moments later, Aimee was standing in the doorway. "Come on in." She held the door open and gestured for me to go in ahead of her.

I tossed the magazines to the side, grabbed my bag and entered the room. It was small, but neat. There were no pictures on the walls. A white board hung with a handwritten quote that changed weekly.

Today's quote was by Charles M. Blow: *One doesn't have to operate with great malice to do great harm. The absence of empathy and understanding are sufficient.*

I chose the chair instead of the couch. The couch was too Freudian for me. We sat across from each other.

"So, what's going on?" she asked. She settled into her chair with a notebook and pen in hand.

"Do you think that's true," I said pointing to the quote on the white board.

"Absolutely. Bad behavior has more to do with suffering and less to do with malice. Typically, narcissists are suffering immensely, and this suffering is the catalyst that leads them to inflict pain on others. At their core, they are quite damaged individuals. The media spends so much time villainizing narcissists that we tend to forget they're hurting too. Hurt people hurt people, and their kind that causes the most destruction, carries the most pain inside. Anyone who can hate so much and thrive off inflicting cruelty to others must be a sad, tortured soul. We need to understand that no amount of love given to them will fill that empty void inside. They'll continue to take it unmercifully, unaffected by their behavior on others, because in the end, they're creatures that, although self-loathing, exhibit a strong sense of self preservation."

"I've been thinking about Erik and his moments of rage. I remember having a conversation, something would set him off, and then he'd go from luke-warm to boiling within seconds."

"Okay. What did you do when this happened?"

"I tried to stay calm and diffuse it. If I didn't, it could get out of control."

"Why do you think you felt like you're responsible for his emotions and behavior?"

"I don't know. I felt bad for him because he had so many issues that he was working through. I felt like if I could help him, then maybe we'd get to a good place."

She paused to write something in her notepad before speaking. "What makes you think you have so much power to right the wrongs of the past and determine the course of the future? You're placing a heavy burden on yourself."

I didn't know how to answer that question. "I remember he told me that his rage originated from a childhood trauma. It made me think of my own experiences in childhood. I shared things that happened to me. He wanted to know every detail. I felt like he was trying to understand me better and that it was a way for us to connect on a deeper level. He never went into detail about what happened to him, so I didn't really know the whole story. After that, when we fought, he would go back to my childhood trauma and use it against me, throwing my confessions in my face. It's like he wanted to shame me for things that I trusted him with. I don't understand why he wanted to hurt me with something that was so personal."

"You know what, Dana. We don't even know if what he told you was true," Aimee said, leaning forward, allowing me to take in her statement. "Often these types…that is, those who suffer from antisocial personality disorders like narcissism and sociopathic behavior, weaponize information you give them. They disclose a small piece of information with you to gain your trust. Their objective is to lower your defenses and build confidence. That's what predators do. They gain information and then use it to exploit you."

"Not true?" I asked in shock. "You mean he might have made the whole thing up?" I couldn't imagine. It had never even crossed my mind that any of the childhood trauma that he had shared with me could have been lies.

"It's quite possible, Dana."

"But why would someone do that? What would be a reason for lying about that?"

"It opens you up to manipulation and control."

———✖✖✖———

Erik insisted on coming to the media visit at the hotel. He had some things to do at his apartment and couldn't go up on Friday. He promised to meet me on Saturday. I arrived on Friday evening. I had done so many of these before that I didn't mind being alone. It gave me a break from all of the Erik drama.

I could breathe again, even if it was for a short time. That night I went to dinner by myself and enjoyed every minute of the solitude. For the first time in a while, I slept peacefully on the plush king-sized bed and woke up rested. In the afternoon, I went for a relaxing spa treatment. Erik messaged me and said that he'd be there by dinner. The dinner reservations were for six. When he hadn't arrived by five, I called him. He had some story as he always did, saying that he had car trouble, and how could I have been so insensitive to not understand that he had to get his tire fixed. What if he had driven on the bad tire and gotten into an accident? It would have been my fault. How could I be so selfish to not care for his well being? It was really an art form how Erik could twist a simple phone call about being on time to me wishing bodily harm on him.

Then he threatened to not even come. I should have seen it for a sign and taken him up on the offer, but part of me still thought there was something to salvage. The universe was basically holding up a sign written in red ink and capital letters, reading *THIS IS A SHITSHOW. PLEASE STOP*. But of course I didn't. I told him that I could change the reservation to seven to accommodate him. Like this trip was about him. I noticed that there was a pattern of behavior: every time there was something that had to do with me, he would do his best to sabotage it and make me miserable. This event was no different.

Still a no-show at seven, I went to the restaurant alone.

Thirty minutes later, Erik sauntered in, rolling his carry-on behind him, and sat across from me at the table.

"Hello, daaaling. I need a drink."

My eyes rolled, past practice had confirmed that his personality and alcohol didn't mix well, not to mention with the adderall that he shouldn't have been prescribed. I tried to smile, but I was already pissed at him for accusing me earlier of being selfish, showing up late to dinner, and now demanding a drink. I sat in silence.

"Cat got your tongue," he said, taunting me.

"I ordered already," I said, deliberately ignoring his attempt to bait me into an argument.

I looked around the room. Erik watched me and stopped on an Italian guy a few tables away.

"Are you wishing that you were with him? He's your type, isn't he?"

"Erik, stop. You haven't even been here for ten minutes, and you're already starting with me. Please, just drop it."

"I have no idea why you're with me. I can't believe I rushed to get here, and you have the nerve to stare at that guy behind us."

"Erik, please keep your voice down. I'm not staring at anyone. I was just looking around the room."

"You're making a fool out of me."

The waitress arrived with a variety of dishes. Erik ordered a drink. Minutes later she came back to deliver his drink. He tossed it back effortlessly.

"You're such a fucking cunt. I'm sick of you and your disrespect." His voice grew louder.

"That's it," I said. "I'm not going to sit here and listen to this. I invite you to dinner, and you can't even act right. I'm not going to sit here and have you cause a scene. We're done here."

I motioned for the waitress. "We have a change of plans. Can you wrap this up and I'll take it to go?"

Moments later, doggie bag in hand, I was out the door. Erik trailed behind me, rolling his carry on through the hotel, following me.

"I don't know why you're following me. You've already ruined everything."

I walked through the hotel. He followed me up the elevator and to the room. He was quiet and pensive, like he was plotting his next attack. I got inside the room and poured myself a glass of wine. I earned it after having to put up with my terrible dinner guest.

"Can I have a glass?" he asked.

"I'd rather you not. It doesn't mix well with your personality."

He quickly snatched the bottle and threw it across the room like he was a rock start intent on destroying the hotel room.

"Are you fucking kidding me," I said, watching the red wine splatter on the carpet and the white curtains. "GETTTTT OUUUUUT." I said pointing to the door.

Thankfully he left, satisfied that he had caused enough damage. As soon as the door closed, I wept on the floor. I got some towels and warm soapy water, and on my hands and knees, I cleaned the carpet and curtains. Once again, I was cleaning up his mess. He was like a tornado that destroyed everything in his path.

CHAPTER 16

Erik's temper was out of control. His episodes happened so often that I got used to the behavior like a parent who anticipates her child's outbursts. It became part of our normal routine. *There goes Erik again.* I had it down to a science. Disengage. Nod in affirmation. Fix face to express sympathy. Apologize. The whole cycle was becoming less and less appealing as the days passed by. It was all so exhausting. He was ill. That was one thing that was certain. The extent of his illness I never could have imagined. Even though I had become unwillingly accustomed to his tantrums, this time felt different. The source of his rage was an anonymous email I received.

Thanksgiving and his birthday had passed relatively uneventfully. By this point, I had been walking on eggshells for a while and knew how to navigate around his mood swings to prevent setting him off. I assured him that the Thanksgiving dinner he cooked, which tasted like he dropped an open container of salt, wasn't salty at all. I choked down the sodium-filled meal with a smile. He got up every morning as if he were going to work. His job was to fix the bathroom, but what started as just a broken window that needed replacing, became a full renovation that he wasn't capable of performing, yet not ready to admit that he was unskilled and unprepared for the job. He kept up with the illusion that he intended to complete the bathroom, but he and I both knew that wasn't the truth.

After a day of work, I came home to yet another day gone and no progress made. I stopped nagging him about it, because it only made him angry and blamed me for it. The days were getting colder and darker. The threat of having to be stuck in the house with him throughout the long winter months loomed over me. I took it day by day, sometimes hour by hour. My plan for the evening was to finally get some sleep. I lay in bed, checking my phone. An email from an account that read *Erikbeckerexgirlfriend* appeared. I clicked on it. The message began: *It has come to my attention that you are currently dating Erik Becker. You need to know that he is a consummate liar. His wife is not dying. He is a deadbeat dad, ex-husband, and has a terrible temper. I am worried for your health and safety.*

This wasn't going to be the calm evening I had hoped for. I wouldn't be getting any sleep after all. Who was this anonymous woman?

In the email, his ex-girlfriend warned me about the man that I had fallen in love with, detailing accusations of abuse, adultery, deceit, and destruction to women. Her tone was startling.

> *To: contact@danabuckmir.com*
> *From: erikbeckerexgf@gmail.com*
> *Subject: Erik Becker*
>
> *Hi there,*
> *It has come to my attention that you are currently dating Erik Becker. You need to know*

he is a consummate liar. His wife is not dying. He is a deadbeat dad, ex husband, and has a terrible temper. I am worried for your health and safety. Don't believe me? Have a look at the links below. They highlight the current cases, his convictions, as well as his financial troubles. If you want to date him or try to save him, go for it. He will suck the life out of you, lie to you, take your money, get you drunk every time he wants to have sex. If that wasn't bad enough, I hope he does not hurt or frighten you. He has stalked friends and ex-girlfriends like me in the past to the point where I inquired about a restraining order.

Just wanted to help out another woman from making the same mistakes I made. Don't walk – run from this man!!!!

One of Erik's Ex's…

She even went so far as to attach links to court cases as proof of his atrocities. After reading the email, I started shaking. My mind went back and forth on whether I should respond to her, and what I would say if I did. I decided it would be better to not engage with her, and just go directly to the source.

I went downstairs to confront Erik. Standing in the kitchen making dinner, he looked up from stirring the pot, "Hey babes."

I didn't know how to present the information, so I just blurted it out, "I just got an anonymous email from a woman who claims to be your ex-girlfriend, and she doesn't have nice things to say about you."

He didn't look shocked, which should have proved to me that he was guilty. He continued to stir the pea soup, unfazed by the news.

"Another one?" he said nonchalantly.

Any normal person who was accused of something so appalling would be outraged. But in his defense, he didn't know the details yet, and yes, there had been another ex-girlfriend that reached out to warn me about him a couple of months before.

I thought back to the message from Beth only a month into our relationship: *Dana, I'm warning you right now about Erik. Please be careful. He's dangerous. You don't need to be abused.*

"What does the email say?" he asked. I read him the email, feeling like I was running out of breath as I uttered each word. When I was finished, he shrugged and said, "Dinner will be ready in fifteen minutes."

My mouth opened in disbelief. "Did you just hear what I read?" I asked, shocked by his cavalier attitude.

"Send me the email. I'll look into it," he said, turning away from me and searching on his phone, I assume for the email. "I didn't get it. Did you send it?" he asked.

"I will. I will, but I'm trying to understand why you aren't saying anything to me about it."

"Like what? What do you want me to say? You already know most of those things about me. It's nothing new."

"I do? No, I don't think I know these things. What I do know is that you should be doing something to make me feel better about it, but instead you're acting weird." I fidgeted nervously. I was having a perfectly good night for once. It was drama free, and then I got this email, and now I don't know what to think."

Perfectly good night? Who was I kidding? I couldn't even get one night of peace.

"I don't know what you want me to tell you. It's obviously another scorned woman who's jealous of our happiness. She probably saw my post about our Thanksgiving together and wanted to try and drive a divide between us. I don't get these cunts. Why don't they just go play with their vibrator or eat a pint of ice cream instead of reaching out to you?"

"Erik, you have to take some accountability for this."

"She's just trying to hurt you, to hurt us."

"No, Erik. She's not the bad guy. I asked for your honesty and you fed me betrayal. I asked for your loyalty and you gifted me with deceit. This is what happens when you hurt people. Your ex-girlfriend didn't hurt me. You hurt me. Own it."

"Believe what you want," he said, leaning for a pack of cigarettes and digging his fingers into his pocket, frantically searching for a lighter. "Where's my lighter, Dana? I had four lighters, and now I have none. Where do the lighters go? Do they just get up and walk away?"

"I don't know. Maybe someone stole them." I immediately regretted that last statement.

"Stole them? Are you trying to be funny, Dana? Do you think this a time to make jokes? I'm over here getting persecuted by some scorned woman who is trying to ruin my reputation and our relationship, and you want to make light of it. This is what I'm talking about when I say that you're selfish and you don't care about my feelings."

"I'm sorry, Erik." I wondered why I was apologizing. As women, we are programmed to apologize to make everything better to fix the situation. I did nothing wrong, and my default was to say I'm sorry.

"You're fucked up, Dana. Everything is a joke to you. Plenty of fucking laughs, right? You don't care about anything. You don't care about how this is making me feel. You question me instead of taking my side. You're supposed to love and support me, but instead you don't trust me. It sounds like you believe this bitch's lies. Maybe it's because of your childhood. That's why you're so numb. Which parent fucked you up more? Was it your mother or your father?"

"Erik, don't turn this around on me. We're talking about your ex-girlfriend and an email, and now it's about me not caring and my childhood? Let's have some perspective." I looked in his jacket pocket and handed him the lighter. "Here. Where are you going? I want to talk about this." He walked past me, coldly opening the back door. He put on his shoes, the cigarette now in between his lips.

"What did I tell you about asking questions that you already have the answers for? Where am I going? It's pretty obvious that I'm going to have a cigarette. You're the dumbest smart person I know. You have three degrees, but you can't even deduct that I'm going to have a cigarette when you see a cigarette in my mouth, I'm asking for a lighter, and I'm walking outside?" he said, looking at me with disgust and closing the door behind him.

I opened my phone and tapped on my author email and reread the message that set this night on a downward course. A few minutes later, Erik walked back in the house, a peculiar smile on his face. His eyes had transformed from a raging storm to a gentle breeze.

He kissed me on the forehead tenderly and held my face in his hands, "Baby, I'm going to need you to call up whoever runs your domain and trace the IP address for the email," he said gently, which I realized momentarily was only because he wanted something.

"Erik, I'm not doing that."

"Why not?"

"Because it's disturbing enough that I was sent this email. I'd rather not get involved. This is your issue with your ex. I didn't sign up for this circus. I don't want it to interfere with my life anymore."

"I'm not surprised you would react that way. You're always taking someone else's side. Why wouldn't you want to help me track down the cunt that is doing this?" The storm had returned in his eyes. I could never understand how he could switch so quickly from what seemed like a caring soul to an unrecognizable monster.

"You need to calm down. I'm not the enemy here." *At least he's calling someone else a cunt for a change*

"When you don't want to help me, you are the enemy. It makes me wonder if you sent the email."

I looked at him in disbelief because the idea was absurd. "If I sent the email? Are you fucking kidding me, Erik? What motivation would I have to send this email to myself?"

"I don't know, but you don't seem to care about finding out who did, which makes me wonder."

"You're crazy. I can't believe that you're putting this on me," I said, rolling my eyes and walking upstairs to the bedroom. No good was going to come from standing there arguing over something that he was now accusing me of being a party to.

I let some time go by as a cooling off period and went downstairs to make tea. He was sitting on the couch. His right, middle, and index fingers were in his mouth frantically chomping on his nails. His left hand was holding his phone as he intently focused on something. He did that when he was deep in thought and stressed.

He looked up from his phone. "Baby, come here for a second," he said, cheerfully motioning for me to sit beside him on the couch.

A suspiciously innocent smile swept over his face. I wondered what version of him I was about to encounter, since just moments before I was the enemy. Nothing with him was what it seemed. His moods changed unpredictably. I prepared myself for round two of Jekyll and Hyde.

"What are you doing?"

"I'm trying to trace the IP address for the email. I found the last 4 digits of the phone number. Now I'm going through my contacts to see if anything matches."

"Why are you even bothering, Erik? Like why does it matter? What are you going to do if you find out who it is?" I asked, desperately trying to make sense of his behavior.

It was becoming more and more common for me not to understand why he did the things he did. Why he ripped apart the downstairs bathroom when he was just supposed to replace the window? Why he flipped from calm to enraged within seconds? Why he said he was going to do something and did the complete opposite? It was enough to drive anyone crazy. I was starting to believe that that was his intention. To either drive me crazy or make me think that I was. Aimee said she wasn't surprised I couldn't figure it out. *How can you possibly think that you'll understand crazy when you're not?* Her words resonated in my head. I'd been trying so hard to translate a language that I didn't speak.

"Because this bitch is going to pay. I'm going to prosecute her to the full extent of the law and charge her with harassment," he said, clenching his fists into balls so tightly that the color from his fingers disappeared to only show white knuckles.

I was surprised he changed up his usual term for women from "cunt" to "bitch."

"I think you should let it go."

With vengeance in his eyes, he said, "Not a chance. She's going to pay."

I leaned over, peering at his phone screen to see that he had stored the email in a folder he entitled *Dead Meat* and chills ran down my spine. Dead meat? He sounded like an eight-year-old that got picked last for kickball and was intent on punishing someone for the rejection.

The realization set in that this man would never let anything go. It was becoming clearer that being on his radar was probably the worst position to be in. It was a relief to have someone else in the line of fire instead of me, yet inadvertently I was always caught in his cross hairs.

I put my head on his shoulder. He stroked my hair with one hand and continued to scroll on his phone with the other.

I closed my eyes for a moment and remembered a time when things were fun and new, and more importantly, drama-free. A time when we sat on the beach, the sun burning our faces, the laughter blowing in the breeze as I ate strawberries and listened to him read excerpts of my book aloud in different accents. Those were blissful times, the ones that made me fall for him so quickly. And just as fast as they came, like waves crashing violently against the rocks, the tide brought them in and quickly dragged them away. The ebb and flow of our relationship provided one constant like the ocean tide. It was always turning and uncontrollable. Placid one moment, violent the next. There was no predicting the force or intensity. The worst was the undertow that could pull me under without warning. I couldn't fight it. Within seconds I was at its mercy, flailing my arms and legs, kicking back to regain balance amongst the chaos. Fighting it was futile. I longed for that familiar tide to return in the same condition as I remembered, but it was lost to the vast unknown abyss in which I found myself treading water, trying to stay afloat. Those days seemed like eons ago and there was no indication that they were ever coming back.

CHAPTER 17

An uneasy feeling sat like a weight in the pit of my stomach, and even though he reassured me that, "everything would be okay," I knew that it wasn't going to be okay. He had repeated those words like a mantra after every episode almost like he was trying to convince himself that they were true. He and I both knew differently. The word *promise* was meaningless at this point, because he had overused his promise card. I mean, how many times can you break a promise without the word losing meaning? "I promise I'll be home in an hour" resulted in him being home three hours later with some elaborate story of all of his tools falling out on the highway, or his debit card being flagged for fraud, or his phone dying and he couldn't find a charger anywhere in civilization. Too many fabricated stories – and I thought I was the storyteller. He told them with such conviction that they were almost believable. But I knew better that there was no way he was the unluckiest guy in the world. He was just shady as fuck. "I promise I won't disrespect you again" came with another barrage of insults. I learned quickly that the word *promise* bore no worth, because he so flippantly dispersed them without any follow-through.

"Why would you promise to do something and not do it? I asked one night. "It makes your promises meaningless when you can't follow through with them." To which he would apologize and then say he'd do better.

"I promise I'll try harder. I'll do better, my love. If there was anyone in this world I'd ever want to change for it would be you."

I rolled my eyes because I had heard it all before, and albeit he seemed so sincere in this moment, I knew it wouldn't last. It was only a matter of time before he fucked it up again. That was one promise he could keep. Part of me felt like he didn't give a fuck, and there were no real consequences for not following through with promises, so why bother? The other part of me accepted that maybe he didn't have it in him. Something was severely lacking with his moral compass of evaluating right and wrong and living by the societal standards of agreed upon behaviors. An impending feeling of doom set in, and I knew that things were going to get much worse.

The next day started off unceremoniously, but I came to realize that uneventful mornings didn't guarantee peaceful days. Erik's mood swings were becoming more and more frequent. He seldom slept. When he did, it was for short periods of time. He would mumble in his sleep indecipherable utterances that led me to believe that he was tortured by something. I heard him pacing back and forth at all hours of the night, mentally wrestling with demons that I had the displeasure of becoming acquainted with. A few times I thought he was talking to me and realized he was talking to himself. Full blown conversations, as if he were answering a voice in his head. The situation was growing more frightening as he escalated on a larger scale.

Each time, it was mentally draining to endure his long winded tangents, getting in my face and screaming. His attacks were always at night when I was just about to fall asleep or in a deep sleep. They were initiated from falling asleep during a movie, to a picture that I posted on social media from years before I met him.

"Dana, wake up." He roused me and shook my shoulder.

"What is it, Erik?" I opened my eyes to him staring at me, wide awake. "What time is it?"

"Why do you always fall asleep during a movie?"

"I don't know. Why would you wake me up to ask that?"

"Well, if I'm not sleeping. You shouldn't be sleeping."

"Come on, Erik. I'm tired. I just want to go back to sleep." I rolled over, trying to tune him out and drift back to sleep. I should have known that wasn't the end with him. He wasn't satisfied until I was alert and engaging in some type of conflict with him.

"It makes me feel like you don't want to spend time with me when you fall asleep when we're watching a movie. Don't you see how that makes me feel?"

I searched his eyes for some form of empathy, but what I found was cold and empty.

"Don't you see that you're a pain in the ass right now and I just want to go back to bed? I don't want to argue with you. It's 1 A.M. I'm tired. Show a little compassion, and leave me alone if you see me sleeping."

"I'm sick of you only caring about yourself. You're so selfish. I don't know how you can't see how hurtful your behavior is. My therapist says that falling asleep early is neglectful of our relationship."

"My sleeping is hurtful to you? I can't with you, Erik. Fuck you and fuck your therapist." I put the pillow over my head and closed my eyes, hoping he would just go away.

He continued relentlessly, and what started as him being upset about me falling asleep during a movie, escalated to me partying in South Florida, all of which eventually escalated to him calling me a whore. It always went there.

"I bet when you were in South Florida you didn't go to bed at 10 P.M. I bet you were out partying, probably just getting to the bar then. 'Cause you were out fucking everyone in Fort Lauderdale."

"Erik, you're ridiculous. I don't know how you go from feeling lonely to calling me a whore. Just don't engage with me." I jumped out of bed not wanting to be anywhere near him. I grabbed a pillow and blanket and walked out of the bedroom intent on sleeping on the sofa downstairs. Anything to get away from him and his vile mouth.

"Why are you getting mad at me? No one told you to date everyone in Fort Lauderdale."

"Fuck you, Erik." I screamed. "Fuck. You." I stormed downstairs.

Silence ensued, until minutes later he called down sweetly, "Baby, you don't have to sleep downstairs. "You can come back up."

"Oh, that's so nice of you to give me permission to sleep in my own bed in my own house," I said sarcastically. "I'm fine down here. Just leave me alone." I slept curled up in the fetal position on an uncomfortable sofa that was not meant for sleeping, with my dog tucked up against me, praying that was the end of it. He had won and gotten what he wanted, which was to disturb my peace and make me feel uncomfortable, to let me know that he had the power and was in control. Everything was about showing his dominance and maintaining that he had the upper hand. If he had control over me, he had an illusion of power that fueled him.

I usually didn't last the night on the sofa. He would come down and kiss me on the forehead and ask me to come upstairs with the promise that he would leave me alone. In the morning he'd act like it never happened. I'd open my eyes to him smiling and gazing lovingly at me, an almost eerie manufactured look on his face

"How did I get so lucky to wake up to another day with you?"

I would forgive him, because how could I not? I wanted everything to be okay.

"You're my heaven, angel. I love everything about you. You're perfect. We're perfect together. I can't wait to marry you so we can wake up like this together for the rest of our lives."

I knew it was wrong, and most of the time he was so over-the-top with professing his love, that it seemed disingenuous. But I wanted to believe it was real.

He got up, made me a cappuccino, and delivered it to me in bed. "Here you go, princess. Don't get up. Just stay and rest. I'll feed Lucky and take him for a walk." These were the moments that I waited for. The calm after the storm where I was pampered and adored. They didn't last long. Soon he would be having an episode again. It continued in that way, the push and pull, the extreme highs and lows. It was enough to drive anyone crazy.

CHAPTER 18

The torture lasted for a while and escalated. I felt like a prisoner trapped in my own home. He spewed insults vehemently. *Cunt* was by far his favorite; after a while I got used to it. I was desensitized from it so much that I wouldn't even react when he said it to me. It was almost more of an annoyance than an offense, as if I was irritated that he couldn't produce any new material. That his vocabulary was so limited to the same narrative with the same sprinkled-in words was beneath me. The reel kept repeating like one of those tea cup rides at an amusement park where someone keeps spinning it, and you just want to get off because it's not fun anymore and definitely wasn't worth the three tickets and thirty-minute wait in line. I gave up. I became complacent. A lot of my reaction or lack thereof came from my years as a teacher in the inner city school system. I had disciplined myself not to react to situations that people generally had a response to. I was conditioned to be stoic and unaffected if a student screamed in my face, because as professionals, that was what we were supposed to do. Never could I have imagined that my training would be applied to my personal life.

One morning, Erik was on some tirade about something.

"Cunt bitch. I don't know who messed you up more, your mother or your father," he said.

When he calmed down, I tried to talk with him about it. "Why do you think it's okay to call me names and bring up things about my childhood? I've asked you before not to do that, but you continue to do it."

There was always an excuse for his behavior, ranging from childhood trauma, to frontal lobe formation, to misdiagnosed mental illness and inadequate medication.

"My therapist told me that my frontal lobe is weakened and that it grows more challenging at the end of the day to make rational decisions when it becomes harder to control."

I was supposed to get on board with the fact that his abuse stemmed from the formation of his frontal lobe, and it just sounded like one big cop-out for horrific behavior.

"Dr. So and So says that a lot of behavior stems from my childhood trauma. My mother was verbally abusive, and my father was physically abusive. Fear in childhood transforms to rage as an adult."

I sat there and listened to him because I cared about him and I felt sorry for him, but honestly it was a bunch of bullshit. It was pretty evident that he had conned his therapist and was trying to con me.

"I don't know, Erik," I said. "You're an adult. You can't blame your problems on your upbringing anymore. You get to an age where the direction of your life is a result of the actions that you take, and it's no one's responsibility but your own."

Of course, he was very agreeable, but he didn't change. He rationalized hitting me on the boat as a result of his undiagnosed Intermittent Explosive Disorder. I entertained his self-diagnosis for a bit, and then I realized that was just another opportunity to remove obligation for his faults.

"I wonder if I can walk around calling people names, raging out at any moment, having no control over my emotions, and then blame it on Intermittent Explosive Disorder," I said. "It sounds like that's just another name for being an asshole."

I was at a loss with how to help him and got wearier by the day. At this point love wasn't enough, and my patience was growing thin. He wasn't working, so he had a lot of ideal time on his hands. His car had just broken down, so he had no way to leave the house. His unemployment checks were spent quickly with shopping sprees on Amazon. The days were growing darker and colder, and I dreaded being stuck in the house with him for the upcoming winter months. I felt like I was dancing a tightrope, trying not to trigger him.

The rages were becoming part of our routine. He couldn't go more than a day without flipping out about something and taking it out on me. I was always to blame. If I moved something and he couldn't find it, that was my fault. If I had a bad day and entered the house in a bad mood, that was my fault. Things started becoming my fault that weren't even close to being my fault. If he banged his head, that was my fault because why was the board hanging so low? If he left his cigarettes outside overnight and they were soaked by the rain, that was also my fault because he brought them in, and I must have brought them back out on purpose. If his car wouldn't start, that was my fault too.

And of course he took zero accountability. Why would he? He was too busy making me accountable for everything to ever consider that he was a participant. It was an endless battle of push and pull. Like a constant roller coaster of emotions, a hamster wheel, a yoyo, which made me dizzy and exhausted.

Tuesday morning I went to work with my students, and he stayed at the house per his usual schedule of drinking coffee, smoking cigarettes, masturbating, going on social media, and pretending to fix the bathroom that he had destroyed.

"I promise that when you get home, the bathroom will be finished," he said.

It was hard for me to keep a straight face, since I had heard that promise every day for the past few months. Instead of him making progress with the bathroom, it seemed that every time I opened the door he had ripped something else apart or dismantled something else. I never signed up for a bathroom remodel. I simply asked him to replace the window that he broke. That request turned into him tearing out the walls, insulation, wiring, removing the toilet and sink vanity, all of which he did without my permission and while I was sleeping. Then he locked the door so I couldn't even see what was happening inside the bathroom that was no longer a bathroom, but just bare walls – more like an outhouse than anything.

The bathroom was a point of contention. Every angle I chose to address it backfired. If I left him to his own devices, he accomplished nothing. If I nagged him, he took his anger and frustration out on me. If I tried to motivate him, it was pointless. If I asked him questions, he would get irritated. I tried to take the matter into my own hands by suggesting I hire someone, to which he shot down and said that we'd have a problem if I did that. I knew that meant that I wouldn't hear the end of it.

So I was at his mercy. I started paying attention to him more. He was researching and making videos of his supposed "bathroom remodel" filled with disillusionment, believing he could teach himself how to do it and perhaps make a business out of it. He was seriously misguided, and if he wanted to be successful at any business, it would have been demolition because that's the only thing he knew how to do well. He had years of practice in that department.

CHAPTER 19

"Just leave me alone, Erik," I muttered groggily.

My wish was for once to be able to sleep through the night without being woken up and subjected to interrogation or an impromptu therapy session. Nighttime was the hardest. When the sun came up he was a different person. Like the night brought out the monster and the day chased it away. The past couple of nights he'd rouse me from a deep sleep, almost as if he had waited until I looked content and peaceful, my body finally relaxed from a day filled with tension. I would murmur softly, sputtering out the stress with each exhale. He'd shake me repetitively until I had no choice but to wake, because in his eyes, I wasn't allowed to sleep.

During these tirades, he'd pontificate about something I was suspected of doing, as if everything was a big conspiracy against him. He would hit me with a barrage of questions half asleep, to which he was never satisfied with the answers. I couldn't escape him. He wouldn't stop regardless of how much I cooperated or pleaded. It wasn't about his accusations or my answers after all. It was about power, and he wasn't going to give his up any time soon.

EVERYTHING WILL BE OKAY

"Eriiiiiiik, I need sleep." I opened one eye to see his crazed face hovering over mine. His eyes flared, wide pupils dilated. The light from his cell phone illuminated in the darkness. I turned over to see him staring at the phone, studying something intensely. One hand gnawing at his nails, the other hand stuffing chocolates in his mouth. A nearly empty bag of candy sat beside him. Plastic wrappers were sprinkled around the bed. I put a pillow over my head, hoping that I was dreaming, but soon realized that this was a waking nightmare. One that reoccurred regularly. I knew now what it felt like to experience sleep deprivation. It wasn't like the type a mother sacrifices to nurture her newborn, but more like the type cadets experience in military training intended to break down the individual and make them conform. This was an act of aggression. Part of his psychological warfare.

Waking me was never for anything reasonable. Perhaps there was a fire in the house. Or maybe he hurt himself and needed help. Although I secretly wished that he would have an unexpected accident. I fantasized about that often. He would be a one-liner that I told friends at a dinner party. After pouring a little more wine into my glass the host would ask, "So whatever happened to that guy you were dating?" "Oh, that guy." He would forever be nameless. That guy. "He had an accident and went away." As if it were that simple. I'd take a sip of the liquid, letting it warm my throat and laugh casually, completely at ease knowing that he was merely a footnote in my life. A hiccup based on a bad judgment call. A distant memory that, as time went by, faded more and more until it was unrecognizable. When someone asked his name, I might not even recall it because that guy was so insignificant, he barely left an imprint on my psyche. I couldn't be that lucky though.

Sometimes Erik would wake me because he couldn't sleep. "If I'm not sleeping, neither are you," he'd say. "I bet you weren't sleeping by nine when you were partying in South Florida," he'd continue. Most of the time he was triggered by something he saw online. He would wake me up because he saw something on social media that set him off. A friend commented on my post or put the heart emoji instead of the thumbs up. As if I had any control over what emoji someone chose to use on social media. He found a picture of me and a guy from ten years ago and wanted it taken down. It was always a male friend that he was threatened by. He wanted to know the entire history of our relationship. How did I know him? How often did we talk? Did I ever have sex with him?

"Of course you had sex with him," he would say. "Haven't you had sex with everyone? Do you know how embarrassing this is to me?" He was very concerned by what other people thought.

It never ended. He scrutinized pictures of me. Why was I posing that way? It was too provocative. I must be starving for attention. The insults and accusations were incessant. Erik trusted no one. He was overly suspicious. Looking back now, I realize the suspicion originated from his own fear of what he was capable of. If he was doing it, everyone else must be too.

In the beginning I made the mistake of arguing with him. I pleaded my case, stating that I was allowed to have male friends. He didn't have the right to tell me that I couldn't be friends with an entire gender. When that didn't work, I tried to rationalize with him. The photo was taken before we even knew each other. How could he possibly get mad at that? I assured him that he didn't have to worry, especially considering that I was the faithful one in the relationship.

Finally, I tried another strategy, drawing upon the lessons I'd learned in school about the Suffragettes. I channeled my inner feminist, proclaiming that I could wear what I wanted and speak to whomever I chose. After all, he didn't own me. Erik laughed in my face and proceeded to tell me how much of an attention-seeking whore I was. His cruelty was limitless. He called me so many names it became a regular part of his com-munication style, almost like his love language. I didn't react to the words anymore. The sting that they initially left had faded a long time ago. Now, I was numb. Aimee once told me that the mind has a way of protecting itself by shutting down.

I stopped saying "don't call me that."

I stopped crying.

I stopped fighting back.

Why did it matter? He never listened. They were just words anyway. I got so used to him calling me names that I didn't even flinch when I heard them.

"Is there anyone you haven't slept with, you filthy whore?

"Would you like another cup of coffee?" I said as if he merely asked if I had slept well.

I didn't even bother getting upset. I doubt he listened to or cared about my beliefs. He always won and, in the process, wore me down with each interaction. I'm sure that was his intention.

When all options had been exhausted, I started complying just to shut him up. I'd agree with him even though I didn't actually agree with him. How dare I wear a bikini at the beach? He was right. I should be more sensitive to his needs. I'd take a picture down or unfriend someone on Facebook just to satisfy him. He was right. I shouldn't be friends with half the human population. I soon realized that my attempts to appease him were futile. He couldn't be pacified. I'd give him a little. It wasn't enough. He wanted more.

Sometimes I even entertained his rants.

"Why do you act like this?" I'd ask desperately seeking an answer.

His mood would soften, hearing me take an interest in the inner workings of Erik, which gave him a platform to rattle on about his theories. He'd blame his mother who emotionally neglected him and his father who physically abused him. Many times, it seemed as though he wanted the same answers that I did, and he grasped for anything to explain his own behavior. He had a whole lot of theories with no real solutions. Maybe he needed more therapy. Maybe his frontal lobe was weakened. Maybe he was on the wrong medication. He poured himself into researching psychological articles, often psychoanalyzing himself and others in order to sound informed enough to be able to persuade his psychiatrist to write more prescriptions and convince him of his newest theory to explain why he was broken. Nothing would fix him.

His latest: Intermittent Explosive Disorder. He tried to convince everyone who would listen that this was why he behaved the way that he did. It just sounded like another excuse to me, or a way to gain pity for his "disorder." In my mind he was just an asshole with an anger problem. No disorder was going to justify that.

The only card I had left to play was to ask him to leave. Of course, he'd refuse. His entitlement was shocking, since it was my house. Erik made it abundantly clear that he wasn't going anywhere. My feelings didn't matter, so I accepted that I was being held hostage in the house that my father left me. The house that I paid for. My house. Like a stealth assassin, Erik had slowly infiltrated the property and taken me captive. He was physically there, but even more menacing was that he had hijacked my mind. I was at his mercy.

Sometimes I slept in the living room just to get away from him. It infuriated me that I was forced to sleep on the couch in my own house. As pay back, the next night I locked him out of the bedroom. He pounded on the door. The wood shook like it was made of paper. He was the Big Bad Wolf and I was one of the scared little pigs. When I refused to open the door, Erik became innovative and removed the doorknob so I couldn't lock him out.

I reached out to God during those nights, begging him to make it stop. As if God could come down and *poof* – Erik would be gone. I bargained. If he got rid of Erik, I would be a better person. I'd volunteer at the shelter. I'd give back to my community. I'd donate money to all of the charities I saw on television with the sad-looking dogs and the starving kids in Africa.

God didn't answer my prayers.

All the Our Fathers and Hail Marys couldn't save me from this monster. One time, I left and just drove around in my car, hoping that when I got back, he would be gone. Maybe God had finally answered my prayers and poofed him out of existence. That was never the case. He was always there. Erik's wrath was unrelenting. Both he and I knew the truth. There was no escaping him.

CHAPTER 20

The routine carried on that way for so long, it made me start to doubt that it was ever different. He was like a ticking time bomb. An emotional terrorist. I tried not to set him off. The push and pull was the only constant in our relationship.

I was living with a big secret that I was ashamed to share with anyone except Aimee and Mia. I didn't want to hear anyone say "this isn't the Dana I know," like I was a big disappointment. It was easier to isolate than to explain or lie.

I moved on autopilot, mentally and physically exhausted. I was skinny. I had lost almost thirty pounds within a few months. It wasn't healthy. My body was in a constant state of fight or flight. Everyone said I looked great. I didn't feel great. I hardly ate. I chain smoked cigarettes and drank more nights than I would like to admit. To turn it off. To make it go away. To stop the noise. To escape the madness.

The woman I saw in the mirror, skeletal, drawn and lifeless, was not the vibrant self-assured one he had met. In a short time, he'd robbed me of my confidence.

My mother abstains from alcohol, but that didn't stop me from ordering a glass of cabernet midday. We met at a little

Italian restaurant in the center of town known for their tapas and wine selection. The occasion – a belated birthday lunch.

"Can I get a hug?" she asked.

I stood up and fell into her embrace, not realizing how much I needed one. She held me longer than usual, and at that moment, I wasn't a 40-year-old woman. I was a 4-year-old child who wanted her mommy to make everything better.

"You're skinny, Dane," she said, feeling the bones in my back as we hugged. Like many mothers, mine gets pleasure from feeding me.

"I know," I nodded. "It's from stress."

Some people overeat when they're stressed. I've always done the opposite. I completely lose my appetite and can drop twenty pounds easily in a short time. For the past three months my body has been running on adrenaline in a constant state of fight or flight, and it's noticeable in my appearance. I take a sip of wine to calm my nerves.

The server came over. "Are you ladies ready to order?" My mother and I looked at each other.

"Can we have a few more minutes?" I asked.

He smiled, "of course. Take your time."

"So what's good here?" she asked

"Honestly, everything is good. I really like the scallops over risotto, and the gnocchi with butternut squash is heavenly," I said, pointing to the items on the menu.

"Ooh, those sound yummy," she said.

"Really, you can't go wrong. What are you in the mood for?"

Food is very important in our family, and ordering the correct item like it's our last meal has always been a tedious production that starts with considering one thing, going through the entire menu of options, and then circling back to the original choice. Lately, the last meal concept has hit home from more of a joke to a possible reality with Erik's behavior escalating. It makes me think that I should pay careful attention to this menu and choose the best item, savoring every bite in case it actually is my last meal.

"I don't know. Maybe I'll just get a sandwich," she said. "The chicken panini sounds good."

The server returned to the table. "Do you ladies have any questions?"

"I think we're ready," I said, looking at my mother for confirmation.

She shook her head, "I'd like the chicken panini with a side salad instead of fries. Dressing on the side."

"Good choice," he said. "Is the house vinaigrette okay?"

"Sure."

"And for you?"

"I'll have the Cajun chicken salad with no red onion."

"Great! I'll put that right in for you," the server said, taking the menus away and leaving the table. As soon as he left I took another sip of wine.

"I always ask to leave out the red onion. You can never get that taste out of your mouth, no matter how much you brush your teeth or use mouthwash," I said, realizing that I was talking about onions to avoid the topic of conversation that my mother wanted to have.

Discussing bad breath from onions is much easier than the discussion about what happened on the boat. She was patient, and I could tell that she was waiting for me to start. She didn't want to push me in fear that I might shut down.

"So your brother told me that you talked to him about what happened to you on the boat. What's going on with that, Dana?"

I guess I didn't expect my brother to keep the information I had disclosed a secret. That was a burden he didn't need to bear. I hated to see her look at me that way. So disappointed with the woman I had become.

"We're working on it."

"But what if he doesn't work on it?"

What if? The what ifs were something that I didn't want to think about. It was embarrassing enough to talk about it. So I pretended that everything was okay. I made our relationship out to be a fantasy when people asked. It was the relationship that I had imagined it would be. I've met my soulmate. Who could argue with that? I isolated myself from people when I didn't want to lie. Pretending that I was so busy that I couldn't accept an invite from a friend – eventually the invites stopped coming. It was too much work to have to pretend, and I already had a full-time commitment dealing with Erik.

Erik kept promising me that it would get better. It never did. It just got worse. He was good at making promises he couldn't keep. That was about the only thing he was good at.

⎯⎯⎯✼⎯⎯⎯

I was having a hard time processing the question that my mother raised at lunch, and my appointment with Aimee couldn't have come sooner. Her office was simple, yet inviting. A bookcase in the corner. Some landscape paintings on the walls. The lamp in the corner shed light on the dreary day.

I sank into the plush chair by the window. A tissue box sat on the table beside the chair. I pulled a tissue from the box and brought it to my face wiping tears that had formed in the corner of my eyes.

"I don't know why I'm like this," I said. "I'm a fucking mess."

"Why do you feel that way?" asked Aimee, taking a sip from her coffee cup, placing it down and picking up a notebook and pen.

I looked out the window at the raindrops that had collected on the glass. A few blurry figures ran across the street, quickly getting out of the storm into the safety of their cars.

My tears streamed down like the rain, "I can't stop crying."

"You're doing great," Aimee said. "You might not realize it, but you are. This is a safe space. It's okay to cry. You're probably so used to being on guard when you're around Erik, that when you come here, it's a time for you to release and let go."

I looked forward to our weekly sessions. The topic at hand was loving someone who was incapable of loving anyone. When I wasn't talking to her, I felt like I was pretending. Going about my life as an actress with some big secret that I wanted to share, but couldn't. I wondered if people could see it when they looked at me or hear it in my voice. *Who is that girl in the abusive relationship? Why does she stay? Stupid girl.* Like I had it written on my forehead identifying myself to the world. I had changed. I was an imposter of myself. A shell of who I once was.

CHAPTER 21

That night, I realized that we're all just one wrong move away from losing everything.

The storm had finally calmed from the night before. Erik walked into the bedroom chewing on his nails, the dirty gray bathrobe tied around him like he was a vagabond Hugh Hefner.

Without any regard for what I was doing, he announced, "I'm going to need you to respond to the email."

"I told you that I don't want to get involved. This is your issue, not mine."

"Leave me alone."

He took a seat next to me on the bed, picking up my father's computer. I had lent it to him to get his business going, but all he used it for was to go on social media, watch porn and deep dive into my father's life, searching through his pictures and anything else he could find to use as ammunition.

"I want you to tell her that if she doesn't stop spreading lies, you're going to the police."

"Erik, you have the email. Why don't you respond? I'm busy." I was in a writing flow. Finally the writer's block had lifted. With nearly 50,000 words in my manuscript, I was on my way to completing the second book. I didn't need any more interruptions.

"You don't have to be a bitch about it. I just don't understand why you can't help me. You're never on my side."

"Erik, your ex-girlfriend sent me an email with pretty crazy accusations, and now you're giving me a hard time. I honestly don't want to deal with it. It's your problem."

"Cunt," he mumbled under his breath.

"What did you say?"

"I was talking about the email."

"You know what, Erik. When I met you, you said you wanted to make me feel safe. You wanted to be a knight in shining armor to swoop down and rescue the broken girl who was grieving a loss. Guess what? The villains in the story aren't the ones lurking in the darkness, they're the ones that look at you with eyes filled with emptiness. The villains are the ones sleeping in your bed, making you feel safe while they're stabbing you in the back. You're not the hero in the story. You're the villain."

"Oh, wow. So poetic. Save it for your book, Dana. No one cares."

"That's it. Give me my father's computer." I reached for the computer, but instead Erik grabbed it with two hands and slammed it hard on the wood floor. The plastic splintered, the screen cracked and went black.

I screamed, "You broke my father's computer! Get out."

He jumped off the bed. "Gladly. I can't wait to get away from you." A crooked smile of accomplishment plastered his face.

"That makes two of us."

Erik started packing his clothes, throwing them into crumbled balls inside his suitcase.

"I'm not leaving until I take everything."

I left him alone and went back into the bedroom. Pieces of the broken computer lay on the floor. I picked them up and examined the damage. I pressed the button. The light didn't come one. The screen had ripples, indicating that more than likely the damage was beyond repair.

"You're going to pay for this," I said, carrying the broken computer into the room where he was packing.

"Good luck with that," he said callously.

I noticed that he had some of my things in his suitcase. "Erik, those are mine. You can't take my things with you."

"The fuck I can."

I snatched my nightgown from his suitcase. The fabric hung outside of the opening, making it easy to pull.

He grabbed it back and stood up. Towering over me at least 7 inches and almost 100 pounds, the height and body frame that once made me feel safe was menacing. He squared up and pushed me back hard in the chest. I fell to the ground. Images of the boat flashed in my mind. He had hit me once – there was no way in hell I was going to let him do it again.

"This is how it's going down, Erik." I said, pushing myself up.

His nose was only inches away from mine. I could feel his breath exhale on my face. I searched his eyes, but they were empty and cold.

"I promise you, Dana, this isn't going to end well for you." He grabbed my shirt and pushed me aside. His eyes looked lifeless and empty. The emerald color was wiped clean, leaving a bottomless darkness. Vacant. A predatory black lake of nothingness.

I walked downstairs, put the tea kettle on and prepared a mug with a tea bag, trying to think of what I should do next to avoid his wrath.

Lucky ran frantically up and down the stairs, stirring the anxiety in the air.

"Lucky, come here." My voice shook. I didn't trust Erik and didn't want my dog near him. I scooped Lucky up in my arm. The other hand, I used to pour the tea. Remembering the house key on his keychain, I slipped it off the ring, put the key in my bag, and returned the keychain to the holder hanging by the door.

I looked at my phone. He had been packing now for thirty minutes. My anxiety level was increasing.

I yelled upstairs, "Erik, are you almost done? How much longer?"

"Fuck you, cunt. Don't rush me."

"Is it necessary for you to call me names?"

"Yes, it is. By the way, I don't love you. I hate you. I fucking hate you," he screamed in a howl, and I was pretty confident the neighbors heard.

There was something different about him that night. I wrestled with calling the police so many times before. I had always talked myself out of it, convincing myself that I could handle it. This time I had had enough. I was done protecting him. I had to protect myself. He felt so entitled to come into my house, call me names, destroy my property and take his time getting out. I wanted him out now. With every minute that passed, the danger increased. Who knew what he was capable of? I paced back and forth. I gathered my oversized purse. The only contents were my keys, license, a debit card, lip gloss, my phone, Lucky, and my mug of tea, and I walked to the car. I walked back inside the house at least three times and finally decided that the mood of the night left me no choice but to call the police. I debated going back for my computer, but didn't want to press my luck. By this time, Erik's rage was escalating. He was slamming doors and screaming. I needed to get out of there and fast.

I dialed the three digits that I had wavered on dialing countless times within the past few months. The operator answered.

"State the nature of your emergency."

"My boyfriend is acting violent and refusing to leave."

"We've tracked your location. Officers will be there shortly."

I waited in the car parked across the street from my house. Two police cars arrived. One officer approached my vehicle. I rolled down the window. "He's inside the house. He's being violent and refusing to leave."

"Will he act aggressively with us?" the officer asked.

"Probably."

"Does he have a gun or weapon?"

"No. The backdoor is open."

My phone buzzed. I pressed the envelope to see a message from Erik.

You called the police. You fucking cunt, I hate you!

I put the phone down and focused my attention on the officer approaching the back of the house. I watched the officer go up the steps to the back door. The other officer stayed in the front. He hadn't even gotten inside when I heard the glass break, and a blue blur scurried away down the back steps and into the front yard, taking cover behind the police car. "Shots fired. Shots fired."

I floored the gas and drove away. I drove in circles around the neighborhood. He didn't have a gun. He must have thrown something out of the window and startled the officers.

Another message from Erik appeared.

You have a few windows to fix.

I could hear the taunting tone through the message.

Minutes later my phone rang. "Hi, Dana. This is officer Julio. I'm going to need you to come back."

"I'm not going near the house."

"Can you meet me in the parking lot down the street?"

"Okay," I said, turning the car around.

By the time I got to the parking lot close to the house, the streets were blocked. The number of police cars had doubled, and the news had arrived.

"I'm Officer Julio. I'll be taking care of you tonight."

I turned the heat on higher inside the car. He stood outside wearing gloves and a winter hat. I could tell he was cold as he rubbed his hands together. I could see his breath in the air.

A trailer pulled up, and a bunch of officers exited dressed in SWAT uniforms, with helmets, and heavy artillery. One approached the car with a clipboard. "I have a layout of the house." He showed me the sketch. "Are there any exits other than these that are labeled?" He used his pencil to point to the exits marked.

"No," I said, shaking my head in disbelief that this was my life and not a movie. Erik had said in our initial correspondence that we'd star together in an action movie. He had gotten his wish.

The lights from the command center illuminated the parking lot. The media was told to get back, and barriers were put up.

My phone rattled on the dashboard above the steering wheel. Officer Julio had instructed me to leave it there and not answer it. He didn't trust me, so he kept a careful watch.

"I'm not going to answer the phone," I said.

I clicked on the envelope indicating I had a text message

If you don't give me the password of your computer I'll break it. Say goodbye to your precious writing.

I knew I should have gone back for the computer. I thought about all of the work I had put into my book was gone.

"He's been in the house for almost two hours. Have you gotten an update?" I asked.

Officer Julio squeezed the side of the radio attached to his left shoulder. "Any updates?" He listened and reported back. "They said he's closed off all of the windows. He's upstairs in the bedroom."

"He's going to break into my computer. Can't you do something about it? Why does he get to sit inside my house and do whatever he wants?"

"Our objective is to make sure that everyone goes home safe tonight. Right now it's a waiting game."

The phone buzzed again. This time a picture message from Erik of my leather ottoman lodged in the wall going upstairs.

I'm going to barricade myself in your house. I'm never leaving. Oops, the ottoman got stuck in the wall. Guess you're going to have to repair that too.

I showed Officer Julio the picture. "It looks like he's using furniture to barricade himself upstairs."

"We have a detective on the scene who is talking to him through the window."

"Can you ask for another update?"

"The detective said he's coming out."

We waited minutes that felt like hours. And then, another update.

"False alarm. He's not coming out. What kind of game is this? Why don't they just go in and get him out?"

"We don't know if he has a weapon. He's broken a lot of glass. Right now it's only damage to the property. We want to keep it that way."

"Easy for you to say. It's damage to *my* property. The longer he stays in there the more damage he's going to cause. And you want me to just sit here and wait?"

Officer Julio was silent.

A message request from a made up account came up on my notifications. I clicked on it.

The name read Sigorney Weaver with no profile picture. I didn't think the actress would be contacting me. It was Erik.

I'm going to burn the house to the ground. That's how much I hate you.

"What does it say?"

"He said he's going to burn the house to the ground" I jumped out of the car, unable to sit any longer. "You can't let him do that!" I cried hysterically.

Officer Julio radioed the information.

"They're going to cut the gas. Don't worry. We'll inform the company now."

Don't worry. If there was ever a time to worry, I think that time was now. Officer Julio was big on not worrying and waiting. At least he was consistent.

The one-sided texts continued for hours, and finally they stopped.

My phone sat on the dashboard of the car. A silent reminder of our lost connection. Then, another call. Officer Julio shook his head to remind me for the twentieth time not to answer it.

"I know, I know," I said. "I'm not going to answer."

I looked at the screen to see a picture message of a large shard of glass from one of the broken windows followed by a text from Erik and read the words aloud.

I'm going to kill myself in your house. Then you'll have two Daddies die here. I'll take pleasure in haunting you for the rest of your life.

I gasped and dropped the phone, fumbling underneath the seat to pick it up. Suddenly the car walls felt as if they were closing in on me, and the crack in the window wasn't enough. I couldn't breathe. I needed air. I opened the door and drowned out Lucky's barking when I closed it behind me. As soon as I stepped outside the car, I started crying. This is the first time I allowed myself to cry all night. My chest heaved up and down as I tried to slow my breathing so I wouldn't hyperventilate. My face was wet with tears that kept streaming as I imagined the worst case scenario happening. Having no choice but to keep it together earlier, at this point I was starting to lose it. Officer Juilo didn't know what to say. He just stood silently.

"He's going to kill himself. You can't let him do that," I said desperately. More tears streamed down my face. I wiped them away. My face reddened when the sadness turned to anger. Erik knew that my father had died in that house. He knew that it was a sensitive subject, one that I never fully healed from. He had held me when I cried about it. And now he had ripped open the wound and was using my past trauma as a weapon to inflict more pain.

I needed answers. "What is taking them so long? Why don't they just go in there and get him already." I asked, pleading for an end to this mess.

"I assure you that the officers on sight are highly trained and know exactly what they're doing. We just have to wait it out. Trust the process and be patient."

I couldn't be patient. I paced back and forth and lit up a cigarette out of not knowing what to do with my hands, rather than out of habit. My hands were shaking, partly from the nerves and partly because it was December in Connecticut.

"You must be cold," I said to Officer Julio, trying to take the focus off of me.

"I'm okay, Miss. I have layers on," he responded politely.

"You really don't have to sit here with me."

"I do. It's my job," he said and went back to pretending he wasn't freezing his ass off. A call came in from the dispatch. He held the buttons of the radio and said, "Officer Julio here."

Then a silence and my heart sank into my stomach, expecting them to tell us that Erik was dead.

"Is he alright?" I asked. "What's going on?"

He waited to get the full message and turned to me. "He's coming out. He agreed to come out."

A minute later, Officer Julio received another message. "He's not coming out. He's walking upstairs and smashing more windows."

"What the fuck?" I said. "This is getting ridiculous. Why don't you just go in and get him? You're letting him do whatever he wants."

"We're being very careful because we want everyone to come out of this alive," Officer Julio assured me. That sinking feeling returned, bringing a shadow of doubt to his confident words.

"What have they done to get him out of my house?"

"Well, they offered him cigarettes, which he declined. They also offered him a turkey sandwich." As soon as he said "sandwich" I saw an expression on his face that said he was rethinking sharing this information with me.

"You're kidding me," I said, irritated over the situation. "Maybe he would have come out if they offered him an Italian Combo. Why don't you have someone ask him that?"

"Ma'am, everyone is doing the best they can. Please calm down. You getting upset isn't helping the situation."

"Neither is sitting here doing nothing while that psychopath destroys my home. What kind of circus are you guys running here?"

"I understand that you're frustrated. Again, we're doing the best we can."

"Here's an idea, why don't you ask him to, pretty please with a cherry on top, come out, come out and you promise not to hurt him." I said, shaking my head and opting to shut my mouth so as not to say something I might regret.

Officer Julio didn't deserve my snarky remarks. Afterall, he hadn't done anything except report to work, stand out in the cold and refuse to leave my side this whole night, even though his shift ended hours ago.

"I'm sorry." I said. I was the one that had let this monster into my life. If anyone was at fault, it was me. Taking my anger out on Officer Julio was misdirected. In actuality, I was mad at myself. "This is just all so crazy. I don't mean to take it out on you."

"You're fine, Miss. Don't worry. It will all be over soon."

Officer Julio got a call on the radio. "He's coming out."

I held my breath until the confirmation came over the radio indicating he was in custody. I waited, thinking he would change his mind, but no one followed up with another call. I exhaled a sigh of relief. It was over.

"Can we go back to the house now?" I asked.

"Give them a few minutes."

I drove my car to the edge of the barricades, past the news. Police cars surrounded the house. An ambulance held Erik inside.

"Why is he in an ambulance?"

"They need to evaluate him at the hospital, since he threatened to kill himself."

"I don't think you want to go in there. It's a lot worse than I thought," the officer said.

"I have to see," I insisted.

My shoes crunched on the large and small pieces of glass that covered the steps as I walked up the backstairs. Broken glass. Fractured memories. The back door had been broken down from the police trying to get in. The heat had been shut off as a precaution after Erik had threatened to burn the house down. It was freezing inside. It felt almost as cold as the temperature outside. The front door was gone. It was now just a gaping hole letting the cold winter air into the house. The shelf with my pictures stood in front of me. The pictures frames were broken, the faces had been scratched out. Even the urn that held my dead dog's ashes was shattered in pieces.

I began to cry. I ducked under the ottoman that was wedged into the wall. Upstairs was worse. Every single window was destroyed.He had taken anything he could find to throw through the window onto the yard below. My father's hanging plants that I had kept alive after his death were tossed around. Fragments of the ceramic pots littered on the floor. Potting soil. The thick rope that had secured them had been cut from the ceiling. The walls had large holes that looked like they were caused by a hammer or crowbar.

The room was drenched in darkness. I put the flashlight on my cell phone and scanned the room. None of the light fixtures worked. He had destroyed all of them. The mirrors in my bedroom and bathroom were shattered, as well as the tub and the glass shower door. He clogged the toilet with bathroom products, makeup and shampoo.

The damage was unfathomable. A waft of cologne filled the air. Erik had removed every bottle of my father's cologne from the medicine cabinet and smashed each. No doubt an attempt to eliminate any memory of my father. I walked in the bedroom. A plate of cigarette butts laid on the bed with a tray of graham crackers, marshmallows and chocolate. He was smoking and making smores while destroying my house.

My computer lay on the bed, the last victims of Erik's wrath, completely obliterated into tiny pieces. Years of writing, gone forever.

"This is what happens when you wait. This is what happens when you want to be patient when there's a violent lunatic destroying my house," I yelled to the police officers trailing behind me, taking pictures of the crime scene.

"Ma'am, we did what we had to do. We made sure no one was hurt and everyone could go home."

"Go home. What home?" I asked. "You all have a home to go to. Where am I supposed to go?"

One of the officers approached me. "You had a protective order against him. You should have known something like this would happen."

"Don't you dare," I said. My hand raised in a stopping motion. I looked around at the damage and weeped. "This is what happens when you wait. This is what waiting gets you."

The officers followed me back downstairs. Officer Julio turned to me and said, "I'm sorry. I didn't expect it to be this bad."

I turned to Officer Julio. "Please tell your colleague that he needs some sensitivity training. This is not the time for I told you sos."

"I thought he was going to go there and hoped he wouldn't." I shook my head.

He handed me two papers. One with his name and a case number. The other with a list of domestic violence contact information. I held the paper in hand looking over the information.

"Here's the victim's advocate number. Give them a call in the morning. Do you have anyone you can call?"

I looked at my phone. It was 3 A.M.

"Do you have somewhere to go?"

I looked blankly.

"Can you call someone?"

"It's 3 A.M. I've tried. No one is picking up."

The officers walked away, their uniforms disappearing into the darkness. My pulse was still racing, but everyone was gone now. I was alone. Silence surrounded me. I sat outside for a few minutes, scrolling through my contact list. It didn't make sense to even bother at this hour. No one was picking up. It would be best to wait until the morning and reach out then. I scooped Lucky off the ground and carried him inside. We sat on the couch, three blankets wrapped around us. Glass everywhere. No heat. Both front and back doors were wide open. I shivered and held him tightly. Rocking back and forth I counted down the hours until the sun rose. My mind replayed the night's events. Adrenaline had me wide awake, but every now and then when I began to doze off, I'd hear a rattle that would make me jump. I didn't feel safe. I wondered if I ever would. There was no way I was getting any sleep.

CHAPTER 22

The next day I had an emergency session with Aimee.

"I just thought if I loved him hard enough he would give me what I needed. Instead, he took everything from me."

"He loved you the best way he could."

"Did he, though? I'm not sure he was ever capable of loving anyone, including himself."

"Well, let's make this about you. You didn't do anything wrong. You were the best you could be in that relationship."

"But it doesn't make it hurt any less."

"No, it definitely doesn't. I'm so impressed with your strength. Most people would completely fall apart if they were in your shoes, and no one would blame them for it. Look at you. You're surviving. And, you're doing the best you can. I commend you for it. You could have given up, but you carried on."

"I didn't have a choice."

"Be gentle with yourself, Dana. You've been through a major trauma. It's okay to feel sad and frustrated and disappointed, along with all the other emotions that you're going through. You know, being human is beautiful and confusing, awkward and exciting. It's so many emotions, and most of the time we're all just going through the motions trying to get it right, but what we fail to realize is there's no right or wrong. It's all just part of the experience and it's messy. And that's okay."

"I think what bothers me the most is that he doesn't love me. I just feel so stupid."

"When you love, you love hard. You just wanted to be in love and that's a beautiful thing. The only mistake you made was picking the wrong person. It's not your fault. This is no reflection on you. He is the one with the deficit. Not you."

"I just don't understand." The tears streamed down with more frequency. I reached for a few more tissues.

"He's not capable of love. I know that's something that's hard for you to understand. We can't try to comprehend what is beyond us. It's like a 'normal' person trying to rationalize with a mentally ill person. It doesn't work that way."

"Why do you think he spiraled out of control like he did?"

"You were growing stronger. He was losing control over you, and you were beginning to see him for what he really was, and that made him lose it. It was a constant power struggle, and he wasn't going to let you get away that easily."

"All I ever did was try to help him," I sniffled and blew my nose into the tissue.

"You're incredibly generous with your love. You have an enormous capacity to love and be loved. This is not a measure of you. My concern is the price you paid for it. You were willing to pay extra for love and affection.

"I just don't feel like myself. I feel pathetic."

"My goal for you is to get to a point where you don't need anyone for validation. That you love yourself above others. It's the hunger that you had to be loved that made you susceptible to someone like Erik."

"I don't see that happening any time soon."

"There's no timeline for healing, Dana. And it's not linear. You might feel like a complete emotional wreck today, and tomorrow you might feel stronger, and the next day back to the previous. It's all part of the process, and sometimes we just have to sit with the uncomfortableness of it all. You have to feel it to heal it."

The session was coming to an end. I felt exhausted from all the crying. I sat up in the chair and put my coat on.

"Believe me, you're doing great."

"Thanks," I said.

Aimee walked behind her desk and opened up her calendar. She grabbed a pen from the cupholder next to a vase filled with colorful Gerbera daisies.

"Does 10 A.M. next Wednesday work for you?"

"Yeah, that works."

"Call me if you need anything." She wrote our appointment in the calendar and then looked up, "I mean it, Dana. It doesn't matter what time. Please don't hesitate."

"Thank you."

Aimee walked me to the door. "You've got this, Dana. And I've got you."

———∞———

When something awful happens, you just want to purge it. Because holding it in allows it to fester, and the dirtiness of it takes over your body. You just want to let it out. That way, the darkness doesn't have to live inside of you. Eliminating that darkness makes room for the light to enter through the cracks.

I'd started oversharing with strangers. Aimee said it's a trauma response. Yesterday, I had a forty-five-minute conversation with the Optimum associate. It began with a call to cancel my service. I was fine until Jennie from Arkansas asked me why I was canceling. I could have made up a reason. I switched to another provider. I wasn't happy with their service. It wasn't affordable for my budget.

Instead, I said, "My boyfriend threatened to kill me and my dog and destroyed my house to the point that it's uninhabitable and now I'm living in a hotel." The sentence came out in one long string of unintelligible words, left to sit there for someone else to make sense of.

"I'm so sorry ma'am. That's just awful."

"Thank you."

"Is he locked up? Please tell me you're safe, sweetie."

"Yes, he is. I'm safe." *At least for now.*

I called to make a dentist appointment. I lost it when the woman recognized my voice and asked how I was doing.

Again, I answered with the same response: "my boyfriend threatened to kill me and my dog and destroyed my house to the point that it's uninhabitable and now I'm living in a hotel." Every time, I felt like I was a country singer reciting a tale of woe. All I needed was a pickup truck and a cowboy hat.

I went to the package store to buy a box of wine. The cashier made the same mistake.

"How are you?"

"Well, it's funny you ask. Not so good," I said. He got more than he expected. As did all the people in line behind me, waiting patiently to start their happy hours, while I poured my heart out to anyone who would listen.

Every time I opened my mouth it felt like I was purging something toxic out of my body. If it stayed inside, it would fester like a disease spreading through my organs, ultimately leading to my demise. I had to let it out. With each overshare I felt a little lighter, removing the remnants of the darkness he left behind.

Something that struck me harder than Erik ever could was the kindness that I received from strangers. I once asked Aimee why people responded with so much love and acceptance when I unpacked my emotional baggage in front of them. She said that when I overshared, it resonated with people, even though they may not have experienced exactly what I had.

"We all carry baggage, that makes us able to empathize with others."

Considering what I've lived through, it brought me comfort to know that I was surrounded by more angels than demons.

CHAPTER 23

Erik was prohibited from coming near the house or what was left of it. A piece of paper from the judge said so. I didn't know why he would want to, though. All that was left was just the bones. A skeleton. Like a picture frame with all the glass shattered out, just waiting to be filled. I couldn't even walk inside the house without hysterically crying. I got anxious when I had to stop in and grab clothes to bring to the hotel. My chest tightened and my breath shortened. My thoughts raced and my vision blurred. The first time I felt that way, I thought I was having a heart attack.

"Don't worry," Aimee said. "You can't die from a panic attack."

Even though she assured me I couldn't, it felt like I was dying. And if the panic attack didn't kill me, Erik probably would. The protective order said that he can't come within ten miles of the house. The one that didn't feel like mine anymore. He had made sure of that.

Now I was displaced in a hotel with a front desk attendant who was told not to give my name or room number out to anyone who inquired. I was free and he was in a hospital, soon to be in custody. Why did I feel trapped? Detective Stewart who specialized in working with victims in domestic violence cases said, "You're one of the lucky ones. I'd hate to think what would have happened to you if you didn't get out of the house that night. This could have ended badly." I didn't know how to respond. It seemed pretty bad to me.

The first question people asked when they called to see if I was okay was where I was, and I couldn't tell them anything. I was instructed by the detective not to give out my location, just in case Erik had people who could harm me. I knew very well that he didn't have people. He had burned so many bridges, I wasn't sure he had anyone left that would even give him a ride to the store, let alone go after his ex-girlfriend for retribution. The second thing that people asked was if I was okay, and I couldn't tell them that either. Not because I wasn't allowed to, but because I didn't really know. I looked okay. There was nothing physically wrong with me, but being okay wasn't just about appearances.

Even when I started to feel like I might be, something reminded me that I was the farthest from okay I'd ever been. Right now that reminder was the incessant phone calls from the psychiatric ward. Erik kept calling and I wasn't picking up. Within twenty minutes, he had already left four voice messages, each message more disturbing than the previous.

"The only regret I have is that I didn't cause more damage to your house," he said with a cackle. "I wish I had smashed the windows downstairs in addition to all of the ones I broke upstairs," he continued without an ounce of empathy or concern in his voice.

Venomous words spewed from his mouth exposing pure evil, and I wondered how I ever loved this monster.

In his last message he said, "I'm going to slit Lucky's throat in front of you and let you watch him bleed out. Then I'll pummel you with a hammer until you're a bloody pulp." He spoke in a flat monotone voice, devoid of emotion. At the end of the message he said, "Hope you're doing well. Give me a call if you want to chat."

All those *Criminal Minds* episodes I watched regularly could never have prepared me for that moment when I realized that my ex-boyfriend was just like one of the psychopaths portrayed on the show. It used to fascinate me to watch the stories because they were just that, stories. It felt a lot different when the story was my own.

I called the hospital and explained the situation to the nurse. She apologized and assured me that I would no longer receive calls from him. After hanging up, I got another call from an unknown number, but picked up just to make sure it wasn't him.

"Hello," I said cautiously.

"Hi there. This is Candace. I'm a friend of Erik's. He asked me to reach out to you."

Why would he ask anyone to reach out to me, considering what he had just done? He was in the hospital anyway. He shouldn't have had access to his phone. She said that she wasn't trying to get involved, but that he called her and wanted her to let me know where he was and to make sure I was safe.

About two weeks later she reached out again, saying that she knew this was none of her business, but wanted to check in to see how I was doing and if I had any information on him. For someone that wanted to stay out of it, it didn't make sense that she wanted to know if there was any information about him. I didn't have any information, and if I did, I certainly wouldn't share it with her.

"I'm not trying to impose at all."

Another week went by and she reached out to tell me that she ordered my book and that it'd be arriving on Christmas Eve. She told me that Erik had a cult of very loyal women, but there are also a lot of people who think the situation is fucked up and are willing to help. At this point, she started to win me over. I noticed that it didn't take much – a little flattery and some sprinkled-in support – and I quickly changed my tune about a person.

"You've been very kind and understanding. Cult is the perfect word to describe it. I just can't wrap my head around how a person can blindly follow someone that is so obviously crazy. I have to remind myself that he's had a lot of practice manipulating people. By this time, he must have earned a Ph.D. in deception."

I told her how I had listened to a voice text that he sent me a few days after the boat incident. He was going on and on for five minutes about how he's changing his ways. Talking about how he's done horrific things to women for the past thirty years and wants to stop. How I'm the love of his life. All lies that I'm sure he had said a million times before. You think that if he wanted to change and was cognizant of the behavior it wouldn't take him three decades to do so. Candace shared that Erik had reached out to her a while ago, messaging her about one of his self diagnoses, saying he had borderline personality disorder.

"The more that I talk about this out loud, it makes zero sense that he was opening up to me," she said. "I don't mind that he reached out to me. I will always have my hand out to help someone, but I'm just truly not that close to him. I think I've seen him face-to-face probably four times in the last three years. I can imagine that the Erik that comes out of jail is going to be dramatically different than the one that went in. I just hope it's not for the worse."

She expressed that she wanted to meet up sometime for a walk or just to have a single girl in the area who seems to have similar interests. She continued telling me that she was concerned about me, that she was on my side. At one point she even told me I was her best friend. I soon realized that she had more in common with Erik than I thought. They were both crazy. Every conversation she somehow brought it back to Erik, asking if he was out yet. If I had heard anything. She was very concerned for someone who claimed she wasn't concerned. After Christmas she reached out to me and asked if Erik was getting out soon.

"I can't imagine they can keep him there for that long," she said.

"All I know is what the website says," I said.

"I hope that he's not getting angrier and angrier. When he was in psych ward he told me that he couldn't go to jail and that jail would be the worst place for someone who's tortured by his demons," she said.

"He has a lot of demons to contend with. I wish he would have dealt with them years ago so it didn't have to come to this. He has psychologically and emotionally hurt so many women over the past few decades. Eventually we all pay for our sins."

"It's very scary that he is so manipulative," she said.

Candance kept saying she wanted to meet, but every time I invited her, the plans fell through. After the New Year she contacted me to see how the holiday was and apologized for not reaching out. Even when we weren't on the topic, she'd find a way to incorporate Erik by commenting something about him having good taste in women, or going back to a memory she had of him.

Candace talked to me like I was her friend. She started telling me that Erik was calling her from jail. "I think our lovely friend may have called me three times over the past week or so."

"What makes you say that?" I asked

"I don't answer random numbers really, especially ones that I think are spam, so I've been ignoring an 8-7-7 number. I called it back, and it's some company that helps connect incarcerated people on the phone. But I hung up once I heard that. It was just the beginning of a recorded message."

"Oh, wow. I wonder what he wants from you?"

"Just wanted to let you know. It's only been this week, and I had been ignoring them. Not even sure how he got my number from jail."

"He's acting like you two are lifelong friends. I don't get it. Didn't you just go on a few dates?"

"No kidding. It's really annoying, actually."

"He must have memorized your number. I'm pretty sure they don't allow them to have cell phones."

"Yeah, I don't get his obsession with me as a friend at all."

"It just goes to show you the extent of his mental health issues. Or maybe you made an impression."

"But what could he want? Not like he has time to gossip. I'm not his family. I'm not his lawyer."

"I have nothing to say to him. I can't imagine you would."

"Oh god. I don't."

"Then don't pick up. You don't need any more drama."
Another day went by and Candace messaged me.

I made contact. He sounded weirdly
happy and said he's doing great.

What?

He said that and then the phone cut out.
He called back and said that he
found God and is writing a book.

Found God? How unoriginal.

Yeah, he said he found God in a leaf outside.
He also said that he's incapable of
love, but knows exactly what type of
woman that he wants.

God, I pray for the woman
that he finds.

I just want you to know that my loyalty is to you.
I don't want anything to do with his warped nonsense.

Candance's calls with Erik became more and more frequent. She messaged me after each of them. Maybe she was just
bored, but it seemed like she enjoyed being involved in drama
that she swore she wanted to avoid.

He's literally delusional.
He's loving jail and has no remorse for you.

Loving jail?

He said it's the best thing that's ever happened to him.

That goes to show you how
psychotic he is.

He said it's relaxing, and you don't
need to worry about bills, and you
have a roof over your head.

Wow. Just Wow. Maybe he
should stay indefinitely then.

He's obsessed with you.

What makes you think he's
obsessed with me?

He just always mentions you.

It's really sad when you think
about it. To have no identity
and feel completely empty
unless you're sucking the life
out of someone, or living off of

their accomplishment. Must be a horrible existence.

Totally.

To think that the greatest accomplishment in his for-ty-five years on this planet is that he makes the best margar-ita ever is pretty pathetic.

He's really messed up his life.

I'd hate myself too, if I were him.

He says he's going to make you pay.

I'm sure. Why look within yourself when you can blame someone else, right? That sounds like a threat. Would you be willing to tell that to the detective?

Of course, as I've been saying the entire time, I'm on your side.

I called Detective Stewart and told her what Candace said. She pulled the tapes and listened to the conversation between

Candace and Erik. He hadn't threatened me. In fact, he hardly even mentioned me. So Candace had made the whole thing up. I was shocked. I didn't know which person was crazier. Candace or Erik?

Mia had discouraged me from communicating with Candace. Now, I understood why.

I don't think it's a good idea, girl.

> *What can she do to me that hasn't already been done?*

I don't know. I just feel like she's using you.

> *How?*

To get information. Maybe pass it to Erik.

> *I just wanted to hear her out.*

I think you're so focused on getting answers.
Some things there just aren't answers for.

> *I know you mean well and I love you for it. I have to figure this out on my own.*

CHAPTER 24

I had to run this new information by Aimee and make sense of it. I gave her a quick call explaining what happened with Candace.

"Have you ever heard of a flying monkey?" Aimee asked.

"Not except in the Wizard of Oz."

"That's it. What is the role of the flying monkeys in the movie?"

"They work for the wicked witch."

"Exactly, they do her bidding. From a psychological perspective, a flying monkey is a person that the narcissist uses to do his bidding. Candace is that person for Erik."

"Oh my God. This is crazy. How does that work?"

"The person the narcissist uses is usually someone broken, maybe with substance abuse issues or some unresolved trauma. These wounds make them susceptible for the narcissist to tap into."

"But what's the purpose? What does Erik get from doing this?"

"He gets to connect with you through another person. Also, it's a way for him to retraumatize you. Remember, the narcissist doesn't want to let you go. This is a way for them to keep you in his web, another method to manipulate and control."

"Is Candace aware of what's going on?"

"She may be or she may be so damaged that she believes she's helping."

———— ⠿ ————

I thought it was important to follow up with the anonymous woman that warned me about Erik. The email is what set him over the edge, leading to a domino effect of him spiraling out of control. I often think back to what would have happened if I never got that email. Would we still be together? Would he have destroyed my house? Would something worse have happened? Either way, on my quest for closure, I felt compelled to contact her.

> *To: erikbeckerexgf@gmail.com*
> *From: contact@danabuckmir.com*
> *Subject: Erik Becker*
>
> *Hi!*
> *Above is the link to the article that was in the paper.*
> *There are no words for how I'm feeling. This is truly the worst experience of my life. Thank you for contacting me. I don't want to imagine what could have happened if you hadn't.*
> *With Gratitude,*
> *Dana*

To: contact@danabuckmir.com
From: erikbeckerexgf@gmail.com
Subject: Erik Becker

Dear Dana,

Thanks for sending the link to the article. First and foremost, are you okay?

I would like to keep my anonymity for fear of reprisal from Erik. I only want to help prevent others from falling victim to a con artist and not be humiliated, tormented, harassed, stalked, or made to fear for having a trusting heart. I hope you're able to turn this into a positive and help inform others through your pen (keyboard) on how to look out for predators and the perils of letting your heart listen to the words and not ensuring that it's followed up by the actions.

Best,
A friend

Erik's actions at the house made the paper and the local news. His name was listed. Mine was not. Although my identity could be determined by the name of the street, the town, and labeling me his ex-girlfriend. Anyone with access to social media and the Google machine could figure out that I was the ex-girlfriend pretty easily. I remembered the name of one of the girls he dated before me and looked her up on Instagram.

I copied and pasted the link to the article detailing the 4-hour standoff with police, asking Emma to call me.

"Thanks for calling," I said when Emma reached out.

"Of course. I'm sorry to hear about what happened to you. It sounds frightening. Are you okay?"

"Yeah, physically I'm okay." I never knew how to respond when people asked me if I was okay. I looked okay, but I didn't feel okay. Emotional abuse was hard to describe. The scars weren't visible.

"He has a very dark side and blames it all on his mother. My conclusion is that he really doesn't like women, and his medications are also not the right ones for him."

She continued. "I'm sorry that I didn't warn you about it. I actually thought about it, but he kept posting on social media about you guys, and I thought you were doing well. I hoped that maybe he had healed."

"Unfortunately, not," I said.

"We should meet for a glass of wine sometime."

It was a small wine bar and relatively empty for a midweek happy hour. I took a seat at the bar and waited. A few minutes later, Emma walked in. She was very tall, model-tall, and slender. Her blond hair fell just below her shoulders. Pretty face. She smiled warmly when she approached. We hugged. It felt familiar and comfortable. I liked her immediately. I'm not sure what I was looking for by meeting Emma. I think I was trying to piece together the distorted puzzle, still trying to play detective and get answers as to why this happened to me. I was left with a lot of holes, and I was looking for someone to fill in the gaps. Who better than someone who had spent time with him and had known him intimately? Part of me took comfort in knowing that I wasn't the only one. There was some validation when she shared some of her observations about him.

"He had an intensity about him that was disturbing. We began as friends, but he kept pushing for more really fast, and finally I caved in. Immediately, I knew it was a mistake because he was constantly calling and dropping by the house. Like, he wanted to fit right into my life. He hated my male friends. It got to a point where I felt suffocated. The best thing I could have done was take off. When I went to visit friends in Costa Rica that's when he met you. I just had to get away from him. He had a way of inserting himself into every aspect of your life until you felt like you couldn't escape him. I remember early on when we were just in the friend stage. I told him that I was going out on a date, and I made the mistake of telling him where. He showed up for the date and sat in the corner the whole time, staring at us."

"That's creepy. The behavior you're describing sounds all too familiar. Your decision to leave the country was probably what saved you from his wrath."

We finished our wine. She paid the tab.

"It's the least I can do after everything you've been through."

We walked out together.

"Please let me know if you need anything. I'm here for you."

We hugged and went our separate ways.

———— ⸰⸰⸰⸰ ————

That week, I connected with another one of his ex-girl-friends. She was a friend of a friend.

"I got your number from a mutual friend," Rachel said. "I heard what happened to you and I'm so sorry. I dated Erik a few years back. We met at the gym," she said.

"I think he told me about you," I said.

"Oh, really," she said, her voice raising inquisitively.

"I'm sure whatever he said were parts of the truth or outright lies."

"You're probably right. I want you to know that if there's anything you need, I'm here for you," she said.

"Thank you. I appreciate that."

For Erik, lies were like waves rolling off the tongue. He told lies to get me and more lies to keep me. But eventually, the truth was revealed.

It was a busy week for the past to intersect with the present. After meeting with Emma and talking to Rachel, I thought I'd had my fair share of Erik connections. But then I checked my DMs and found a message from a coffee shop owner who said that she saw the article in the paper. He used to visit her shop regularly. At first he seemed nice enough. He engaged her in conversation and was always pleasant. He was predictable, always ordering the same thing and sitting at a table alone in the back. Turns out he had an interest in some of her young employees and would make comments to them that made them feel uncomfortable. She had talked to him and asked him to stop, and when he was confronted she saw a different side of him than she thought he was capable of. She wasn't surprised when she saw the article detailing that he resorted to violence. He had a scary side, and that day when he had an outburst in her place of business, she saw what he was capable of.

I told her it was interesting, because I had heard about her before. Like many of his stories, Erik had told me a story with an entirely different version of course. He said that he used to visit the coffee shop, and the owner was a lonely woman who took an interest in him. At first he talked to her mostly out of boredom, but when she wouldn't stop with her advances, he told her he wasn't interested. She got angry and asked him not to come into the shop again. He had said this was often a problem. Women were constantly throwing themselves at him.

For the record, I was never romantically interested in Erik at all, although he might have concocted that in his mind. I was interested in protecting my underage employees from Erik's predatory pursuits to cultivate a sexual relationship.

Like many of his stories, I'm not surprised that it held little truth.

The eye-rolling emoji appeared, and I could almost picture her face completely disgusted reading how Erik had completely rewritten the narrative to suit him.

The audacity of this man. He was really delusional to believe that everyone wanted him.

I wrote back with the heart connected to another heart.

He did think highly of himself.
A legend.

A legend in his own mind.

CHAPTER 25

Plywood covered the bare windows and doors. Broken glass was everywhere. A large dumpster in the driveway was filled with debris from the wreckage. Almost a dozen men were inside cleaning the house. It took that many people to clean up the mess made by one man. One monster.

Out of habit I offered the guys coffee, then noticed that the glass carafe was a casualty of Erik's destruction.

"Have you ever seen so much damage?" I asked, still trying to make sense of it.

"Not from a human," one of the guys said solemnly.

"No love, mon. No love," another said with a thick Jamaican accent. The others shook their heads in agreement. With nothing else to say, they continued working, their eyes focused intently on the floor.

Out of sight of the men, I cried. From my experience, men don't know what to do when a woman cries. I didn't want to make them uncomfortable. It was just easier on everyone if I had these mini breakdowns in private. This was a record. I had made it five minutes before breaking down. I cried often, but being in the house was a trigger that brought back emotions. Like a faucet, the tears poured out. I wondered if I'd ever be able to spend any time inside the house without a wave of sadness coming over me.

Aimee affirmed this was normal because I was processing the trauma.

"Tears help us release stress hormones," she said.

Upstairs I passed the bathroom. Two men were delicately removing the jagged pieces of my Jacuzzi tub. What had once been a comforting refuge after a long work day, now was a harsh reminder of how violently things can fall apart. I put my head down and kept walking. In the bedroom, I collected some socks, a pair of slippers, and new underwear. Most of my clothes had been sent off to the dry cleaner, with the hope that soap and hot water could magically remove the marks made from that infamous night. The room felt cold and empty. The only signs of life were downstairs, the sound of drills buzzing and men trudging in and out of the house. My bed was stripped and covered with a plastic sheet. The furniture that was spared from the carnage was moved to the middle of the room so the workers could repair the holes and paint the walls.

The edge of a picture frame peaked out from under the bed. I bent down to pick it up. The glass in the frame was cracked, another casualty from Erik's rampage with a hammer. I broke off the rest of the frame around the picture, careful not to cut myself. It was a selfie he had taken of us while we were apple picking. Fractured memories of what we once were. I remember that afternoon because it was during one of Erik's phases where he promised that everything was going to be okay. We strolled leisurely around the fields, the leaves crunching underneath our shoes. His hand in mine, clenching it firmly like a parent does with a child. Thinking back now, he was always holding on too tightly, imaging his grip as if it could somehow prevent him from losing what was inevitable. That day, he had insisted that the best apples were at the top of the trees since most were picked over or had fallen to the ground. I watched him strain for the apples that were out of his reach. It was his nature to go after the unattainable fruit, but he eventually settled for the ones just below.

After collecting enough to make one of his famous apple pies, we walked through the crowd of people: a seemingly normal couple enjoying a typical seasonal activity on a crisp autumn day. He sang that Taylor Swift song about feeling like an old sweater under the bed until someone came to claim her. And although at the time, I found the ballad to be romantic, I realized later that I had never felt like something that was unwanted or discarded in my entire life before meeting Erik. He had made me feel like I wasn't enough without him, with his disorienting way of loving and loathing me at the same time. As the days transpired, his love for me grew less, despite my wanting more. I ached for just a little affection to sustain me, like an addict does for a drug. His love was my lifeforce. If I could get my fix, I could function. I didn't know who I was before Erik, and I didn't know who I was without him.

In the picture that I held in my hand, Erik was smiling and I'm sure I had been too, but you couldn't tell what I was doing because my face was no longer there. The now amorphous white blob replaced the former features of my face. He had chiseled my image with a knife, first removing my eyes, then nose, and finally my mouth from the photo, until I was an unrecognizable splotch, annihilated by his rage. In an instant, he could vanish me out of existence.

I held the picture closer, inspecting those eyes that I had looked into so many times before: green emeralds sparkling bright. I had seen his eyes change from innocuous to menacing.

How could I not have known this would happen?

Part of me may have known, but never could I have predicted the magnitude of the devastation. It made me wonder if we ever really know the ones we spend our lives with? Or do we only know what side they choose to show us? Folding up the picture, I put it inside the notebook that I carried with me everywhere. The picture served as a reminder that I was stronger than I thought. Right now, it felt like everything was falling apart, but in a way it was all coming together. I was finding myself piece by piece among the rubble. I had survived, and if I could survive this, I could survive anything. Any time I felt weak or hopeless, I would look at that picture and tell myself that if I could live through this psychopath, I could live through anything.

That was all I could take. The visits were brief. It was too intense for me to go to the house because every time I did, I relived the grief and the trauma. Being at the hotel gave me not only a physical distance, but an emotional one that I desperately needed in order to heal.

As soon as I got outside, a rush of cold air filled my lungs, and I could breathe. I opened the back door of the car, tossed the bag inside, and then slid into the driver's seat. Pulling away, I looked back at the house and wondered if I would ever feel comfortable there. As the miles put distance between me and the house, I felt my pulse slow and my breathing regulate.

I used the key card to open the gate and pulled into the hotel parking garage. I had a therapy call with Aimee in about twenty minutes. We had a lot to talk about. The incident stirred about a swarm of emotions. Mostly it was a crippling pain like a vice squeezing my heart and nothing would make it subside.

CHAPTER 26

The many women of Erik Becker were on my mind during my therapy session. Talking with these women made me feel less alone. It also made me realize that this type of abuse can happen to anyone. It wasn't reserved for the Diedres in the world. Any woman could be a victim. The realization was comforting and frightening at the same time.

"Why did Erik repeat the same thing to all of the women?" I pondered during my session. "I keep thinking about the email I got from the anonymous ex-girlfriend – she quoted exact things he had said to me. Like he was reciting a script."

"The script he recited was to get his needs met. It was never about you or the other women. It was always about him. What could he say to get you to adore him? If he told you he loved you, then you'd love him back. It wasn't really love. It was what he had to do and say to get the response he desired. Why would he deviate from that? It was working. It had worked before."

"I talked to one of his victims the other day. She said that she got close with his mother. She confided in her about the abuse. The mother told her to 'toughen up.' I can't believe she would say that to her."

"The narcissist is created from his family life. His parents, the people he trusted, had failed him. We couldn't possibly expect him to trust anyone if he couldn't even trust the only people who were supposed to love and care for him."

"What's the point of all this, Aimee?" I asked, defeated.

"He wasn't your destiny. He was just a chapter in your story."

"I just feel like I'm never going to get over it."

"Trust me. You will. Remember, your current situation is *not* your final destination."

The phone rang. It was Detective Stewart.

"Can you meet me?" Detective Steward asked.

"Can I bring Lucky?"

"Whatever makes you feel comfortable."

Even if she had said I couldn't, I would have anyway. Comfortable is a foreign concept. The only feeling I have is loss. A constant pain in my heart like a vice that grips it until I think that if it squeezes any tighter, it will burst. Then, a release that frees up space for the void of emptiness. That's what heartbreak feels like. I've lost so much in such a short time, and I can't bear to lose anything else. It would break me.

"Did I do the right thing?" I asked.

"What do you mean?"

"Like, calling the police. Should I have? I keep replaying the tape and I really think that I didn't have a choice. I mean. I waited. He escalated. I must have gone out of the house and come back inside five times. My house. Why do I have to leave my own house? I struggle with it because I feel like I could have reasoned with him. I could have calmed him down, but deep down inside, I know that I couldn't."

"You give yourself an awful lot of power that you have the ability to control a mentally unstable person who is violent. So many factors could have contributed to why he acted as he did, but the one thing that I'll promise you is that if you had stayed in that house you wouldn't be sitting here talking to me. He would have killed you. You did what you had to do to protect yourself and your dog. You got out. You followed that little voice in your head and your gut telling you that the situation was beyond your control. And that is the only reason that you survived. Never second guess yourself," the detective said.

She reached for a box of tissues, handing them to me. The idea that he was capable of such violence was frightening.

"In my twenty-plus years on the police force, I've never dealt with someone who flipped so quickly and clearly has no remorse."

"There was something in his eyes that I hadn't seen before. Maybe it wasn't something that I was seeing, but more of an absence. Those green eyes that I had gazed into lovingly so many times. Those eyes that I thought were kind. They were black and empty. I saw nothing. It was frightening. I guess I just find it hard to wrap my head around the fact that I couldn't do anything to stop it," I said.

"Well, it's a good thing you didn't wait around to find out."

"I just didn't think he was capable."

"This isn't an isolated incident. People like this have a lot of practice. I was able to find some information in the computer on Erik. Turns out he has a history of violence in Pennsylvania and New Jersey. I made some calls, and there have been a number of women who reported abuse from him. There were a few instances of intimidation as well, to prevent them from pressing charges."

I shook my head in disgust. There had been many before me, but hopefully there wouldn't be any after me.

"Believe me. You dodged a bullet. You wouldn't be able to sleep at night if you knew the things that people were capable of."

"At this point, I'm not sure that I'll be able to sleep much anyway."

I was searching for safety and protection from a man, and I didn't even realize I was doing it. My father's death had left a gaping hole of unresolved issues. I had lost him as a child, got him back as an adult, only to lose him again.

Aimee believed that on a subconscious level, I was playing out the same pattern with men.

"Your father's absence left a void that you were desperate to fill. This made you vulnerable for someone like Erik to come in and offer you something that you needed. You have to feel safety within yourself, and then you'll stop attracting the wrong men. Only then will you begin attracting men who will add more to your life instead of take away."

Her comment was puzzling, yet insightful. The father-hunger haunted me, driven by the desire to seek love in any form I could get, surviving on breadcrumbs, not needing much.

"Sometimes I just wished he were dead," I said. "Does that make me a bad person?"

"Not at all. It's perfectly normal for you to have those feelings," Aimee said. "A lot of women I work with who have suffered narcissistic abuse feel like they'll never be able to move on unless their abuser is gone. It's self preservation. Death is a way for you to feel some safety. If he's alive, then there's still the threat that he can hurt you. They feel like something has to die before something else can start."

I said what I said in anger, and then I backed off and focused on forgiveness. I didn't want to sit with the anger. I'd prefer to sit with the sadness. The anger would change me for the worse, making me bitter, while the sadness would force me to reflect inward.

"That's exactly it," said Aimee. "You can't seek answers from the ones that hurt you. You have to find them inside yourself. I think you're on the right track. You're doing the work."

CHAPTER 27

I pushed the heavy curtains aside, unveiling the light into a room cloaked in darkness. There were more picturesque views to wake up to: the carved-out mountains etched into the natural canvas at Acadia National Park, or the sun peeking over the horizon shining a kaleidoscope of colors along the Key West coast. Instead, my view was of the police station. I looked down at the building that resembled a fortress and imagined the soldiers dressed in blue were preparing for battle to slay the dragon. Their presence was a reminder that this was not a figment of my imagination. This was real. I wasn't a princess in a castle. I was a resident of room 609 in temporary accommodations.

The hotel room was a little larger than a standard. I had a king-sized bed, leather sofa, and a desk positioned in front of the window. There was a small kitchen equipped with a refrigerator and a two-burner stove. I wasn't sure why there wasn't an oven. The only reason I could think of was that they knew I was a writer and didn't want me to pull a Sylvia Plath. A more realistic reason was that they didn't want anyone to burn the hotel down. People did a pretty good job of almost burning the place down on a weekly basis. The firefighters were called regularly because someone had once again burnt their grilled cheese and set off the alarm.

Everyone had to exit the building amongst the blaring of the alarm announcing repeatedly, "There is a fire in the building. Please evacuate at the nearest exit." Listening to the politeness in the delivery of the announcement reminded me that even in times of potential tragedy, we shouldn't forget our manners.

Guests trudged down the stairs and sat on the sidewalk, waiting to go back to their rooms to do whatever it was that people did in hotel rooms. Finally, we were given the green light and were assured that the only casualty of the evening was the white bread that was burnt to a crisp. There were signs all over, resulting, I assumed, from stupid-people behavior. There was one in the room under the sprinkler on the ceiling. It read: "Do not hang objects from sprinkler," a picture of a shirt hanger accompanied the warning to illustrate the point. Why would someone hang a shirt from the sprinkler on the ceiling? I was better off not asking these questions.

I'd always said that if I ever made it big, I'd live in a hotel. However, I didn't envision it quite like this or under these circumstances. Aimee said that routine was important. I started my mornings at 6:30. I took Lucky out for a walk. Neither he nor I were too keen on Connecticut winters, having spent six years in Florida. I forced myself up before the sun. Outside, the snow banks blocked our path on the sidewalk. Lucky shook from the cold. The Colombian restaurant was open for breakfast. Workers stopped in for a coffee before jumping in their trucks to begin the day. The rehab center across the street had the usual characters standing at the corner, waiting for the bus. Wilberto remembered Lucky and was most likely on his third cup of coffee. He was understandably more animated than I, considering the delay in my daily caffeine boost. Lucky barked at him.

Wilberto responded the same way he did every day. "Tough guy, eh?"

"Little guy syndrome," I said, shrugging and continuing on our walk.

The neighborhood was aligned with historical houses. I looked at each and wondered who lived inside. Lucky lifted his leg to mark every telephone pole on our way. The no trespassing sign hung outside the harbor. No one cared at this time of day. We watched the hues of orange, burnt crimson, and purple pigment stream across the sky. The sunrise was a reminder that even though my life was chaotic, I was surrounded by beauty. With so many uncertainties, I could count on the sun coming up every morning.

We picked up coffee and the breakfast I ordered the night before. My morning routine consisted of waking up, walking Lucky, watching the sunrise, picking up my coffee and breakfast. Aimee gave me credit for just waking up, so everything else was a bonus.

The women at the front desk had become my friends. They all had their own stories of violence. I was starting to realize that the haves were more common than the have nots. I needed to let it out and so I shared more than I typically would. One of the women had a monster who tried to burn her face with a lit cigarette. I will never understand how anyone could try to inflict such harm on another, let alone their girlfriend. She said he was a drinker. As if that's an excuse for evil. It couldn't have happened to a kinder person. She was the first face I met when I checked into the hotel, completely disheveled, barely able to speak, carrying a bag in one hand, Lucky clutched tightly in the other.

She reached for my hand and clasped hers over mine. "Everything will be okay," she said. Though at that time I didn't believe her, I know now she was right.

Christmas didn't look how I had imagined. There was no tree. No presents. No family or friends. Just me and my dog Lucky in room 609. I was a pickup truck short of a bad country song. Even though it didn't feel like a holiday, the television reminded me of the day with a marathon of the movie *Love Actually*. I had already watched it three times and cried every time. Similar to how my life felt stuck in a loop, it was airing again. I kept telling myself that it was just another day, and if I could make it through the next twenty-four hours, it would get better.

There wasn't anywhere to go, so I didn't feel the need to get dressed. A long velour purple robe was my default outfit, more like a uniform that I started wearing daily. I rinsed out a paper coffee cup from the morning. Holding the cup up to the box wine spout, I poured it to the top and secured the lid. I walked around the hotel like Ms. Havershim from *Great Expectations*, wandering aimlessly, looking for the life that had somehow eluded me. Half drunk on box wine, lonely and depressed, I waited for someone to save me, more from myself than from the situation. I quickly remembered that this wasn't a fairytale, and prince charming wasn't coming.

Surprisingly, no one said anything. What could they say? I was that girl who had her house destroyed by her ex-boyfriend, spending the holiday living in a hotel. The women at the front desk were overly nice to me as if they could see the trauma plastered across my forehead, damaged. Aimee said that people had empathy towards me because, even though they hadn't gone through what I had, there was a collective trauma that everyone suffered. She also said that if I got out of bed every morning, I was ahead of the game, so by her standards I was doing pretty well. It didn't feel like it though.

Either way, I was resolved to the belief that I was entitled to a little self-absorbed eccentricity. I had earned that much. I was a writer, after all. Isn't this what writers did? I envisioned Hemingway holed up in a bar on his fifth scotch, penning his classic American novel. Not that I was anything like Hemingway, but it was the same sentiment. If I wanted to drink boxed wine and wander about the hotel in my purple robe, it was my prerogative. I took the elevator from the sixth floor to the third. The doors opened, and I walked out to the parking garage. I pulled a cigarette from the pack, placed it between my lips and lit it. The smoke filled my lungs and I took a sip from my cup. I raised my cup to toast no one in particular.

Looking out at the police station, I remembered why the detective placed me at this hotel. It was a safe haven against all the evil that waited just beyond it's encampment. Would I ever feel safe on my own again?

"Merry Fucking Christmas," I said aloud with a mix of sadness, anger, and profound loss. Then, like the cheap Italian red wine I was drinking, I let my emotions flow. Composure would come another day.

"Have you heard anything from the court?" Aimee asked.

"Well actually, I spoke with the victim advocate the other day. It's a new one of course, because everyone is always leaving or moving."

I could understand why people didn't stay in that role very long. It must be depressing dealing with the judicial system.

"And? Any news?"

"Not really. Just the same thing. He's still incarcerated, and honestly, that's all I care about."

"I worry about how you'll be when he gets out."

"I suppose I have a false sense of security since he's locked up. I really don't even want to hear about it anymore. So much of my life has been about picking up the pieces and cleaning the mess that he made. I've dealt with so much in the past year, and I just want to put it all behind me and move on with my life."

"I don't worry for your physical safety as much as your emotional safety."

"What do you mean?"

"God forbid he tries to contact you."

"I hope he does, because then he'll go right back to jail."

"You've done so much work and you're stronger now, I hope he doesn't find ways to undermine that progress."

"I used to feel so much, and now I feel nothing."

"People with narcissistic personality disorder need closure on their terms. It didn't end the way he wanted it to. I just hope he doesn't try to reach out as a power play to get the upper hand."

<hr />

Time and no contact lifted the fog that I was under. I used to think that I loved Erik, but I realized that it was just control and fear. I had misread the emotions and fell into a dysfunctional relationship, committing myself to it in the name of love. But it was never love. I prayed that something would happen to him, because life would be so much easier for everyone if he wasn't in it. No having to watch my back or look over my shoulder, worrying about a psychopath coming after me with a hammer when I wasn't looking. Everyone would sleep better if we lived in a world in which Erik didn't exist.

There were two sides of Erik Becker. After speaking to him, he'd convince anyone that I'm the villain and he's the victim. I was sure of it. I'd seen him do it. Maybe he was always just one side, and the other was just who he was depending on his audience. Or maybe he never even existed at all. I thought it was real. It felt real. And if it wasn't, I'm afraid I can't even trust my own abilities to know what's real and what's not and distinguish between the two. I loved the sweet side of Erik. The one who brought me cappuccinos in the morning with a saucer underneath the porcelain cup. The one who wanted nothing more than to please me. The one who future-faked a life that deep down inside I knew we'd never have. I tolerated the other side, the evil one, for way too long. The monstrous one that prevailed incessantly until the sweet side soon became a distant memory.

———— ⋙⋘ ————

Aimee's consistency helped with the healing process.

"I'll be here with you through the storm to make sure you make it to the other side. You'll know when it's time to move on from the grief and start a new chapter."

She was the captain navigating through this grief-stricken stage. Like a cheerleader on the sidelines helping me every step of the way, her unwavering confidence that I would survive this trauma made it possible to see some hope at the end of an abyss of darkness.

"I guess what I'm struggling with is if I'll ever be able to put this story to rest and go back to how I used to be. It's consumed so much of me."

"You'll never be who you used to be. This trauma has changed you, and it will always be part of who you are. I think what you need to focus on is controlling your narrative. You are the author of your own story."

As the days went by, I thought about Erik less and less. He didn't consume all of my thoughts anymore. He filled up the quiet space in the morning, the time between waking and dreaming, when I opened my eyes and turned over, expecting to see those big green eyes, that charming smile, and hear him utter the words, "How lucky am I to have another day with you."

The silence enveloped me and the emptiness was oppressive. But I only alloted him that moment. The rest was for me. As I went through the stages of grief and guilt, I felt the sadness and the fantasy of what it could have been. Once I unpacked all of the emotions and laid everything out to examine, once I removed the protective covering and extra layer of plastic underneath, it was all just unresolved love. The love that I wasn't able to get. The love that I was still holding onto. The love that kept me up at night, wondering if I had just done it differently, would I still have had that love? The love that someday I'll share with someone else. It's all just love with no place to go. And I choose love.

Aimee said that Erik gave me the gift of goodbye because I was never going to leave him. And that gift he gave me set me free.

CHAPTER 28

After almost five months of living in the hotel, I checked out of room 609 for good. It was finally time to go home. I entered the house that I had left in chaos and returned to a place that felt different. There was a time when I didn't know if I would ever be able to feel like myself or live in the house again. Moving back was a testament to the human spirit. Resilience. As I walked inside, I felt a wave of calm envelop me. Peace. The demon that haunted the space no longer existed. I could breathe again. It was my own. One that I had reclaimed. It felt like freedom.

Not too long ago, everything was falling apart, and maybe it had to in order to rebuild. Not just physically, but emotionally. I wasn't the same woman that escaped from the house that night. While the windows and walls were being fixed, I had had the time to fix myself. I was once on a quest to find love, and in the process found it within myself. Maybe the gift is in knowing that no matter how shattered a life is, it can be repaired. There is always a chance that something new and beautiful can be created from the pieces. We grow from the wreckage, and with each setback, we begin again. It was like a rebirth. I was reconnecting to so many parts of me that had been neglected.

———— ∞ ————

I thought that meeting with Lauren one more time would bring me some much-needed closure. This time we met at her house instead of a Starbucks. Her embrace was warm and welcoming. We sat on a bench in the backyard overlooking the pond. I handed her a picture of Erik.

"He has a very dark energy." A painful expression appeared on her face as she rubbed her fingers over the picture.

"Is there anything you can tell me about him?"

"He's in prison, right?"

"Yes," I nodded, confirming.

"I feel anger coming from him. He doesn't take any responsibility for his actions. He blames everything on you. Absolutely no remorse."

"I figured that much," I said.

"He isn't going to let this go, either. In fact, he has a lot of time to think about revenge."

"I was worried you would say that," I said.

"Don't worry too much. Things are going to work out for you."

"You know, I was thinking back to when I met you, and my father was talking about the house. Could he have been trying to warn me?"

"Could be," Lauren shook her head confirming. "He just told me that he was with you that night. Although he couldn't prevent the damage from occurring, he was able to keep you safe."

DANA BUCKMIR

A tear rolled down my right cheek thinking about how, even in his absence, my father was watching over me.

I took comfort in knowing that even in death, my father had made good on his promise to always be here for me.

"I want you to do something for me. Get some sage and smudge the house. As you do, I want you to say that if anything inhabits the house other than your father's presence, it must leave. It will be good for you to have a cleansing energy now that you're back in your home."

"How did you know that?" I asked, then realizing who I was talking to, smiled.

"You're a good person. The universe will protect you."

"Thank you."

"You know, there are some people that are always going to be okay, no matter what life throws at them. You, my dear, are one of those people."

She hugged me tightly. A maternal hug. Honest. Caring. When we separated, she looked at me. My eyes were teared up from her words.

"Call me if you need me."

"I will," I said. I looked back one more time as I walked toward my car.

The last image I had of Erik was seeing him in the back of an ambulance. The road in front of my house was blocked with multiple police cars preventing traffic from getting through. After a four-hour standoff with the SWAT team, he had agreed to evacuate the house, but instead of immediately taking him

214

into custody, they were taking him to the hospital. He had threatened to kill himself, which I'm sure was part of his plan to avoid being arrested. The policy stated that he needed to undergo a psychiatric evaluation before they could detain him.

Glass littered the street. I could see that the front door was wide open. It looked as though the police had tried to smash through it. All the windows had been broken. My possessions were strewn along the front yard, exposed for everyone to see. Revealing all of my secrets. I imagine they were used to break the glass in the windows. I walked past the news trucks coming from the nearby parking lot where I had been waiting for it to end. The vultures circled around the blockade, rummaging through the tragedy for the nightly story. Broadcasting my life as if they were entitled to be part of the destruction. Camera men shone lights in my face. Reporters asked me to comment on the incident, to which I had none because there were no words. In their defense, like me, they too were trying to make sense of it. How could this happen? Nothing like this ever happened in our small town.

The police officer escorting me expected that the ambulance would have left already and our paths wouldn't cross. He was wrong. I caught a glimpse of Erik from the rear window. A smug look on his face, almost like a smirk. Then the sirens blared, and the ambulance drove off. He didn't wave because in his mind, it wasn't goodbye. It was so long. Goodbye implied there was finality that Erik wasn't ready to accept. This was "Farewell. Until we meet again." In fact, his last text read that he would come back to "finish the job." The threat was overt. Sometimes at night I'd hear a noise that would startle me out of my sleep and think it was Erik coming back to make good on his promise. Aimee confirmed that a malignant narcissist is fueled by vengeance and won't be satisfied until he gets a finale on his terms. That's not very comforting. As if destroying my house wasn't enough, he wouldn't be satisfied until he caused more harm.

Having time to process everything, I couldn't tell you what Erik looks like anymore. His memory has faded, the workings of my mind trying to protect itself. I couldn't describe him to you if you asked, other than superficial statements. Green eyes. Tall. Crooked nose. I've come to the realization that the reason I have so much trouble identifying him is because identity is exactly what Erik lacked. Erik was nothing and he was everything. He was whatever he needed to be in the moment, depending on the audience and the venue. He was an actor that had acquired a skill, set a long time ago to change like a chameleon and perform accordingly in order to get his needs met.

As a shell of a person, he latched onto his victim, desperate for the supply that he needed to survive. Eventually, his world came crashing down, because the mask would slip and expose him for the con artist that he was. Thinking back now, I couldn't tell you anything I really knew about Erik. Nothing authentic, at least. Who is Erik Becker? I don't even think he could tell you. I fell in love with an illusion. A story that was manufactured. A script that was recited. I fell in love with a lie.

We sit in a circular booth in the back of a posh eatery. The chandelier dazzles with delicate glass, creating a kaleidoscope of color shimmering glints of light around the room. It has been almost a year. I am finally beginning to appreciate the beauty in glass again. A testament to the fact that time does heal.

Six women. The occasion – my birthday. An intimate gathering of beautiful souls sharing a meal and exchanging ideas. We eat, drink wine, and talk about our lives. Where we had been and where we were going. This year looks a lot different from the last.

"Remember your birthday last year?" Mia asks. She surprised me with a visit. Her presence is a gift. And like any good friendship, we picked right back up where we left off, despite the time and the distance.

I answer candidly. "Probably one of the worst birthdays I've ever had." It's incredible how much can change in a year.

Now, I'm sitting with friends. The mood is lighter. There's a warmth surrounding these women. Authentic smiles reflected off the glow from the candles. Laughter fills the air. Abundance. And for the first time in a long time, I feel whole. The me I thought I had lost forever has returned. This is what healing looks like. It feels calm. It feels peaceful. It feels like moving on.

I used to feel so much about the situation, and now I feel so little. Aimee says it's hard to attach an emotion to what I've gone through because I've healed. I've already cried the tears, endured the sleepless nights, the late phone calls trying to make sense of the mess, the detective work obsessing over putting the pieces together to find answers, to which there were none.

The answers that I *have* discovered are: We fall. We rise. We survive. We thrive. I've mastered the first three. Now, I'm focusing on the latter.

I can't think of a better way to celebrate another year older and wiser than to toast to new beginnings. It truly is a celebration of life, because I'm thankful to be alive.

We raise our glasses, connecting to each other, toasting to another year of living, of laughing, of loving. The server arrives with a cake and a single candle, which cues the singing. "Happy birthday to you" fills the air. Indeed it is a happy one. I close my eyes tightly and make a wish. I wish for freedom. I wish for self love. I wish for peace. I open my eyes and blow out the candle.

I don't know what the future holds. I'm not sure anyone really knows. But after this past year, there is one thing for which I'm certain.

Everything will be okay.

Resources For Victims And Survivors of Domestic Violence:
The Center for Family Justice
203-384-9559
www.centerforfamilyjustice.org/
Connecticut Coalition Against Domestic Violence
1-860-282-7899
www.ctcadv.org/
The National Domestic Violence Hotline
1-800-799-7233 (SAFE)
www.ndvh.org
National Dating Abuse Helpline
1-866-331-9474
www.loveisrespect.org
National Resource Center on Domestic Violence
1-800-537-2238
www.nrcdv.org and www.vawnet.org
Futures Without Violence: The National Health Resource
    Center on Domestic Violence
1-888-792-2873
www.futureswithoutviolence.org
National Center on Domestic Violence, Trauma & Mental Health
1-312-726-7020 ext. 2011
www.nationalcenterdvtraumamh.org

CPSIA information can be obtained
at www.ICGtesting.com
Printed in the USA
BVHW041646211122
652449BV00018B/114